Whispers of War

The Untold Stories Behind Nuclear Politics - The Art of War or the Art of Diplomacy

Sam O.A

Copyright © 2023 by Sam O.A

All Rights Reserved. This document is intended to provide accurate and dependable information about the subject and issues discussed. The publication is sold with the understanding that the publisher is not obligated to provide accounting, legally permissible, or otherwise qualified services. If legal or professional advice is required, a practicing member of the profession should be contacted.

From a Declaration of Principles that was unanimously accepted and approved by an American Bar Association Committee and a Publishers and Associations Committee. No portion of this document may be reproduced, duplicated, or transmitted electronically or in printed form. The recording of this book is expressly forbidden, and storage of this content is not permitted without the publisher's written consent. All right is reserved.

The information contained herein is stated to be accurate and consistent, and any liability incurred as a result of inattention or otherwise as a result of the recipient reader's use or abuse of any policies, processes, or directions contained herein is sole and complete. Under no conditions will the publisher be held liable for any reparation, damages, or monetary loss incurred as a result of the information contained herein, either explicitly or implicitly.

All copyrights not held by the publisher are owned by the respective author(s).

The information contained herein is provided solely for informational purposes and is therefore universal. The information is presented without contract or assurance of any kind.

The trademarks are used without the trademark owner's consent, and the trademark is published without the trademark owner's permission or support. All trademarks and brands mentioned in this book are solely for clarity purposes and are owned by their respective owners, who are not affiliated with this document.

For Questions and enquiries contact;

sam@samamoo.com

SA Publishing

Special Bonus

SPECIAL BONUS!

Want These 2 Bonus EBooks For Free?

Get FREE, Unlimited Access To These and All of Our New Books By Joining Our Community

CLICK HERE TO JOIN

Other Books

- How to be More in Tune with The Feelings of Your Customers
- Time Management For Busy People

- Sell Like titans

Table of Contents

SPECIAL BONUS 4

OTHER BOOKS 5

INTRODUCTION 8

CHAPTER 1 12

- HISTORY OF NUCLEAR POLITICS 12
  - *Development of Nuclear Weapons* 12
- DEPLOYMENT DURING THE COLD WAR 18
- KEY PLAYERS AND EVENTS THAT SHAPED THE CURRENT GLOBAL SITUATION 25
- SUMMARY 34
- ACTION POINTS 34

CHAPTER 2 37

- NUCLEAR DETERRENCE 37
  - *Concept of Nuclear Deterrence* 37
- STRENGTHS AND WEAKNESSES OF THIS STRATEGY 40
- WEAKNESSES OF NUCLEAR DETERRENCE: 56
- EXAMPLES OF SUCCESSFUL AND UNSUCCESSFUL DETERRENCE 59
- SUMMARY 78
- ACTION POINTS 78

CHAPTER 3 81

- DISARMAMENT - EFFORTS TO REDUCE AND ELIMINATE NUCLEAR WEAPONS 81
- NON-PROLIFERATION TREATY (NPT) 87
- RECENT TREATY ON THE PROHIBITION OF NUCLEAR WEAPONS 100
- SIGNIFICANCE AND IMPACT: 120
- CHALLENGES TO DISARMAMENT 125
- SUMMARY 130
- ACTION POINTS 130

CHAPTER 4 133

- ETHICAL AND MORAL DILEMMAS - ARGUMENTS FOR AND AGAINST THE USE OF NUCLEAR WEAPONS 133

ARGUMENTS AGAINST THE USE OF NUCLEAR WEAPONS: 134
PRINCIPLE OF PROPORTIONALITY 137
HEALTH AND ENVIRONMENTAL EFFECTS OF NUCLEAR TESTING AND
ACCIDENTS 140
SUMMARY 146
ACTION POINTS 146

CHAPTER 5 .... **148**

DIPLOMACY - ROLE OF DIPLOMACY IN RESOLVING CONFLICTS AND
PREVENTING NUCLEAR PROLIFERATION 148
SUCCESSES AND FAILURES OF VARIOUS DIPLOMATIC EFFORTS 156
IMPORTANCE OF COMMUNICATION AND COOPERATION AMONG NATIONS .. 186
SUMMARY 204
ACTION POINTS 205

CHAPTER 6 .... **207**

COMPLEXITY OF NUCLEAR POLITICS - 207
MULTIFACETED NATURE OF NUCLEAR POLITICS 207
DIFFICULTY OF FINDING SOLUTIONS 214
URGENT NEED FOR CONTINUED RESEARCH AND DIALOGUE 221
Conclusion: *229*
SUMMARY 230
ACTION POINTS 230

CHAPTER 7 .... **232**

SUMMARY OF THE BOOK'S CONTENT AND MAIN ARGUMENTS 232
IMPORTANCE OF CONTINUED DISCUSSION AND ACTION ON NUCLEAR
POLITICS 235
SUMMARY 244
ACTION WORDS 245

SPECIAL BONUS 247

THANK YOU! 248

ABOUT THE AUTHOR 250

O T H E R   B O O K S 252

Introduction

The specter of nuclear war has been looming over humanity ever since the first atomic bombs were dropped on Hiroshima and Nagasaki in 1945. The fear of mutually assured destruction during the Cold War era was palpable, with both the United States and the Soviet Union holding massive arsenals of nuclear weapons pointed at each other. Although the tensions between these two superpowers have subsided, the threat of nuclear conflict remains, with new actors such as North Korea and Iran seeking to acquire nuclear capabilities.

In "Whispers of War: The Untold Stories Behind Nuclear Politics - The Art of War or the Art of Diplomacy", a team of experts tackles the complex issue of nuclear weapons and their role in international relations. The book offers a comprehensive and multidisciplinary perspective on this critical issue, drawing on insights from political science, international relations, history, and ethics.

The book begins with an overview of the history of nuclear politics, tracing the development of nuclear weapons and their deployment during the Cold War. The authors highlight the key players and events that have shaped the current global situation, including the Cuban Missile Crisis, the collapse of the Soviet Union, and the rise of new nuclear powers.

One of the central questions the book grapples with is whether the possession of nuclear weapons is an effective deterrent against aggression. The authors explore the concept of nuclear deterrence, which holds that the threat of a devastating retaliatory strike will prevent an adversary from attacking. They examine the strengths and weaknesses of this strategy, noting that while it has prevented a major war between nuclear-armed powers, it is not foolproof.

The book also explores the concept of disarmament, which has been a longstanding goal of the international community. The authors analyze the efforts of various countries and organizations to reduce and eliminate nuclear weapons, such as the Non-Proliferation Treaty (NPT) and the recent Treaty on the Prohibition of Nuclear Weapons. They assess the prospects for disarmament in the current global environment, noting the challenges posed by the reluctance of some nuclear powers to give up their arsenals.

The ethical and moral dimensions of nuclear politics are

also a significant focus of the book. The authors examine the arguments for and against the use of nuclear weapons, including the idea of a "just war" and the principle of proportionality. They also explore the long-term health and environmental effects of nuclear testing and accidents, such as those at Chernobyl and Fukushima.

Another important aspect of nuclear politics is the role of diplomacy in resolving conflicts and preventing nuclear proliferation. The authors analyze the successes and failures of various diplomatic efforts, such as the Iran nuclear deal and the Six-Party Talks on North Korea. They stress the importance of communication and cooperation among nations in preventing nuclear war.

Throughout the book, the authors emphasize the complex and multifaceted nature of nuclear politics. They acknowledge the difficulty of finding solutions to this critical issue, but remain optimistic that progress can be made. They also highlight the urgent need for continued research and dialogue on nuclear weapons and their role in international relations.

Overall, "Whispers of War: The Untold Stories Behind Nuclear Politics - The Art of War or the Art of Diplomacy" is an essential read for policymakers, scholars, and anyone interested in understanding the complex and ever-changing dynamics of nuclear politics. The book offers a nuanced and multidisciplinary perspective on this critical issue, shedding light on the potential consequences of different strategies and approaches. With the continued development of nuclear technology and the increasing geopolitical tensions between nations, the insights offered by this book are more relevant and timely than ever before.

Chapter 1

History of Nuclear Politics

Development of Nuclear Weapons

The development of nuclear weapons is a topic that has had a profound impact on the course of human history. Nuclear weapons are a type of weapon of mass destruction that uses nuclear reactions to release large amounts of energy in the form of an explosion. The development of nuclear weapons has been driven by a variety of factors, including national security concerns, scientific curiosity, and the desire for military superiority.

The beginnings of nuclear weapons can be traced back to the discovery of nuclear fission in **1938** by German physicists *Otto Hahn and Fritz Strassmann*, and the subsequent work of Italian physicist *Enrico Fermi*, who achieved the first controlled nuclear chain reaction in December 1942 at the University of Chicago. This breakthrough paved the way for the development of nuclear weapons.

During World War II, the United States launched the Manhattan Project, a research and development effort to create the first atomic bomb. Led by physicist *Robert*

Oppenheimer, the Manhattan Project involved a massive team of scientists, engineers, and other experts working at facilities across the country, including the secret Los Alamos laboratory in New Mexico.

The Manhattan Project culminated in the successful test of the first atomic bomb, code-named *"Trinity,"* on July 16, 1945, in Alamogordo, New Mexico. Less than a month later, the United States dropped atomic bombs on the Japanese cities of Hiroshima and Nagasaki, killing an estimated 200,000 people and effectively ending World War II.

Following the war, the United States and the Soviet Union emerged as superpowers in a new era of global politics known as the Cold War. Both countries began a nuclear arms race, developing and testing increasingly powerful nuclear weapons. The first Soviet atomic bomb test occurred in 1949, and the first Soviet hydrogen bomb test occurred in 1953.

Other countries soon joined the nuclear club. The United Kingdom tested its first atomic bomb in 1952, and France tested its first atomic bomb in 1960. China tested its first atomic bomb in 1964, and India tested its first atomic bomb in 1974. Pakistan tested its first atomic bomb in

1998, and North Korea tested its first atomic bomb in 2006.

The development of nuclear weapons has had far-reaching implications for international relations and global security. The threat of nuclear war has loomed over the world for decades, and the use of nuclear weapons in a conflict could have catastrophic consequences for the entire planet.

Efforts have been made to prevent the spread of nuclear weapons and reduce the risk of nuclear war. In 1968, the Treaty on the *Non-Proliferation of Nuclear Weapons (NPT)* was signed by the United States, the Soviet Union, the United Kingdom, and other countries, pledging to work towards disarmament and prevent the spread of nuclear weapons. The *Comprehensive Nuclear-Test-Ban Treaty (CTBT)*, which prohibits all nuclear explosions, was adopted by the United Nations General Assembly in 1996, but has not yet entered into force due to a lack of ratification by several key countries.

Despite these efforts, the development of nuclear weapons continues to be a significant concern in the 21st century. Tensions between nuclear-armed nations, such as the United States and North Korea, and the possibility of non-state actors acquiring nuclear weapons, highlight the need for continued efforts to prevent the spread of nuclear weapons and promote disarmament.

The development of nuclear weapons has led to a complex web of nuclear deterrence and strategic calculations among nations. The possession of nuclear weapons has often been seen as a symbol of power and prestige, providing a deterrent against potential adversaries. This perception has motivated countries to invest significant resources into acquiring nuclear capabilities.

One of the major concerns associated with nuclear weapons is the potential for their use in conflicts. The destructive power of nuclear weapons far surpasses that of conventional weapons, and the use of even a small number of nuclear weapons could cause immense loss of life and have long-lasting environmental and humanitarian consequences. The devastating bombings of Hiroshima and Nagasaki during World War II are stark reminders of the destructive capabilities of nuclear weapons.

The Cold War between the United States and the Soviet Union was characterized by a precarious balance of power, known as *mutual assured destruction (MAD)*. Both sides possessed large arsenals of nuclear weapons, and the fear of massive retaliation acted as a deterrent against direct military confrontation. This balance of power created a tense global environment, with numerous proxy conflicts fought between the two superpowers and their allies.

The end of the Cold War brought about a reduction in the number of nuclear weapons, as both the United States and the Soviet Union recognized the need for disarmament. Several bilateral agreements and treaties were signed to limit the number of nuclear weapons, including the *Strategic Arms Reduction Treaty (START)* and the *Intermediate-Range Nuclear Forces (INF) Treaty*. These efforts led to significant reductions in nuclear arsenals and eased tensions between the two superpowers.

However, the global nuclear landscape remains complex and poses ongoing challenges. Some countries, such as North Korea, have pursued nuclear weapons despite international pressure and sanctions. The proliferation of nuclear weapons and the potential for non-state actors, such as terrorist organizations, to acquire them present significant threats to global security.

International non-proliferation efforts have been aimed at

curbing the spread of nuclear weapons. The Treaty on the *Non-Proliferation of Nuclear Weapons (NPT)* has played a crucial role in preventing the further proliferation of nuclear weapons. It aims to limit the spread of nuclear weapons while promoting disarmament and facilitating the peaceful use of nuclear energy for civilian purposes. *The International Atomic Energy Agency (IAEA)* plays a key role in verifying compliance with the treaty and monitoring nuclear activities worldwide.

Despite the progress made in non-proliferation efforts, challenges and risks persist. There are concerns about the potential for nuclear terrorism, the destabilizing effects of regional arms races, and the emergence of new technologies that could impact the balance of power. The development of hypersonic weapons, for example, poses new challenges to existing defense systems and could potentially undermine strategic stability.

Advances in technology, such as improved precision, miniaturization, and the potential use of artificial intelligence, raise questions about the future of nuclear weapons and their impact on global security. The ethical and moral implications of possessing and potentially using weapons capable of causing such widespread destruction continue to be debated.

The development of nuclear weapons has had a profound impact on international relations and global security. While efforts have been made to prevent the spread of nuclear weapons and promote disarmament, the challenges and risks associated with these weapons persist. The world continues to grapple with the complex issues surrounding nuclear weapons, balancing the need for deterrence with the imperative of preventing their use and reducing the risk of proliferation.

Deployment During the Cold War

During the Cold War, the deployment of nuclear weapons played a critical role in shaping the global balance of power and influencing the strategies of the United States and the Soviet Union. The Cold War, which lasted from the end of World War II in 1945 until the early 1990s, was characterized by intense ideological and geopolitical rivalry between the two superpowers.

Both the United States and the Soviet Union recognized the strategic importance of nuclear weapons as a means of deterrence and leverage in this global standoff. As a result, significant efforts were made to deploy and position nuclear weapons in ways that would enhance their deterrent effect and provide a sense of security.

One of the key aspects of nuclear weapons deployment during the Cold War was the concept of the *"nuclear triad."* The triad consisted of three elements: *strategic bombers, intercontinental ballistic missiles (ICBMs),* and *submarine-launched ballistic missiles (SLBMs).* This triad was designed to provide redundancy and ensure that even in the event of a first strike, at least one leg of the triad would survive and be able to deliver a devastating retaliatory response.

Strategic bombers formed the first leg of the nuclear triad. The United States and the Soviet Union maintained fleets of long-range bombers armed with nuclear weapons, capable of flying into enemy territory to deliver a nuclear strike. These bombers were often on high alert, ready to take off at a moment's notice in response to a perceived threat. Airbases around the world were used to station these bombers, providing flexibility and the ability to project power across vast distances.

The second leg of the triad consisted of intercontinental

ballistic missiles (ICBMs). ICBMs were land-based missiles capable of delivering nuclear warheads across continents with great speed and accuracy. The United States and the Soviet Union established extensive missile silos and underground launch facilities to house these missiles. These launch facilities were heavily fortified and often dispersed over large geographic areas to minimize the risk of a successful preemptive strike. The presence of ICBMs provided a credible threat of retaliation and added to the deterrence factor.

The third leg of the triad, *submarine-launched ballistic missiles (SLBMs)*, brought an additional dimension to the deployment of nuclear weapons. Submarines armed with *SLBMs* could operate undetected beneath the oceans, making them difficult to track and target. This provided a second-strike capability, as submarines could retaliate even if the land-based nuclear forces were neutralized. Both the United States and the Soviet Union deployed nuclear-armed submarines, known as *ballistic missile submarines (SSBNs)*, to maintain a continuous at-sea presence.

Deployment of nuclear weapons during the Cold War was

not limited to the triad alone. Both superpowers stationed shorter-range nuclear weapons in various locations around the world. These included tactical nuclear weapons, which were designed for use on the battlefield, as well as theater nuclear weapons, which had a broader regional reach. These weapons were often stationed in close proximity to potential conflict zones, adding an additional layer of deterrence and strategic influence.

The deployment of nuclear weapons during the Cold War was not without risks and challenges. The world came close to nuclear conflict during several crises, including the *Cuban Missile Crisis* in 1962. The potential for accidental or unauthorized use of nuclear weapons was a constant concern. The concept of *mutually assured destruction (MAD)* underpinned the strategic thinking of both sides, with the belief that the sheer devastation that would result from a nuclear war acted as a deterrent against its initiation.

Efforts were made during the Cold War to limit the deployment of nuclear weapons and reduce the risk of conflict. Various arms control agreements were negotiated, such as the *Strategic Arms Limitation Talks (SALT)* and the *Strategic Arms Reduction Treaties*

(START). These agreements sought to establish verifiable limits on the number of deployed strategic nuclear weapons and promote transparency and confidence-building measures between the United States and the Soviet Union. These agreements aimed to prevent an uncontrolled arms race and reduce the risk of accidental nuclear war.

The deployment of nuclear weapons during the Cold War had a significant impact on the geopolitical landscape. The United States and the Soviet Union engaged in a constant game of strategic positioning, seeking to gain an advantage over each other. The United States established forward-deployed bases in Europe, such as those in Germany and Turkey, to counter the Soviet Union's proximity to Western Europe. The Soviet Union, in turn, stationed missiles in Cuba, which sparked the Cuban Missile Crisis, one of the most dangerous episodes of the Cold War.

The presence of nuclear weapons in various regions around the world had implications for regional conflicts and tensions. Both superpowers sought to influence and deter potential adversaries through their nuclear deployments. For example, the United States stationed nuclear weapons in South Korea to deter North Korea, while the Soviet Union deployed nuclear weapons in Eastern Europe to deter **NATO** forces.

The deployment of nuclear weapons during the Cold War also had profound effects on arms control and disarmament efforts. The fear of a nuclear conflict and the devastating consequences associated with it motivated both sides to engage in negotiations and seek ways to limit the spread of nuclear weapons. This led to the signing of several important arms control agreements, including the *Anti-Ballistic Missile Treaty (ABM)*, the *Intermediate-Range Nuclear Forces Treaty (INF)*, and the *Strategic Arms Reduction Treaties (START)*.

The deployment of nuclear weapons during the Cold War created a delicate balance of power known as *mutual assured destruction (MAD)*. Both the United States and the Soviet Union understood that a nuclear war would result in catastrophic destruction for both sides, and this understanding served as a deterrent against initiating a first strike. The maintenance of a credible second-strike capability was crucial to the concept of MAD, ensuring that even in the event of a devastating attack, the ability to retaliate would remain.

The end of the Cold War brought about significant changes in the deployment of nuclear weapons. As tensions eased between the United States and the Soviet Union, both sides agreed to significant reductions in their nuclear arsenals. The collapse of the Soviet Union resulted in the denuclearization of several former Soviet republics, such as Ukraine, Belarus, and Kazakhstan. The dismantlement of nuclear weapons and the withdrawal of deployed systems became part of the broader disarmament efforts that followed the end of the Cold War.

The deployment of nuclear weapons during the Cold War played a crucial role in shaping the global balance of power. The nuclear triad, consisting of strategic bombers, *ICBMs*, and *SLBMs*, provided a robust deterrent and ensured a retaliatory capability. The deployment of nuclear weapons in various regions around the world added complexity to regional conflicts and influenced strategic calculations. Arms control efforts aimed to limit the deployment of nuclear weapons and reduce the risk of conflict. The concept of mutual assured destruction served as a foundational principle, emphasizing the catastrophic consequences of a nuclear war. With the end of the Cold War, significant reductions in nuclear arsenals and the dismantlement of deployed systems became important steps towards disarmament and reducing the threat posed by nuclear weapons.

Key Players and Events that Shaped the Current Global Situation

The current global situation has been shaped by a multitude of key players and events that have had a significant impact on various aspects of international relations, including politics, economics, security, and technology. These players and events have shaped the dynamics of the global order, influencing the balance of power, alliances, and the resolution of conflicts.

Here, we will explore some of the key players and events that have played a crucial role in shaping the current global situation.

1. **United States:** As the world's leading superpower, the United States has been a central player in shaping the current global situation. Its economic

strength, military capabilities, and diplomatic influence have allowed it to assert significant influence over global affairs. The United States has played a pivotal role in promoting liberal democratic values, fostering economic globalization, and leading international efforts to address various global challenges such as terrorism, climate change, and nuclear proliferation.

2. **China:** Over the past few decades, China has emerged as a global powerhouse, transforming itself into the world's second-largest economy and a major player in international affairs. China's economic growth, technological advancements, and assertive foreign policy have significantly impacted the current global situation. China's Belt and Road Initiative, its increasing military capabilities, and its growing influence in international organizations have raised questions about its intentions and its impact on global governance.

3. **European Union:** The European Union (EU) has played a vital role in shaping the current global situation, particularly in terms of regional

integration and cooperation. The EU has fostered economic integration, facilitated the free movement of goods, services, and people, and promoted a common foreign and security policy. The EU's expansion, as well as its efforts to address issues such as migration, climate change, and economic stability, have had implications not only for Europe but also for the broader global landscape.

4. **Russia:** Russia, as the successor state to the Soviet Union, continues to be a significant player in global affairs. Russia's assertive foreign policy, particularly its annexation of Crimea in 2014 and its involvement in conflicts such as Syria and Ukraine, has raised concerns about its intentions and its impact on regional and global stability. Russia's energy resources, its military capabilities, and its use of hybrid warfare tactics have positioned it as a key player in shaping the current global situation.

5. **Middle East:** The Middle East has been a region of intense geopolitical significance, with various key events shaping the current global situation. The Arab-Israeli conflict, the Iranian Revolution, the Gulf War, the rise of extremist groups such as *Al-*

Qaeda and *ISIS*, and the ongoing conflicts in Syria, Iraq, and Yemen have all had far-reaching consequences. These events have influenced regional dynamics, triggered humanitarian crises, and had a significant impact on global security, energy markets, and migration patterns.

6. **Global Financial Crisis:** The 2008 global financial crisis had a profound impact on the current global situation. It exposed vulnerabilities in the global financial system, triggered an economic recession, and led to significant shifts in economic power. The crisis highlighted the interconnectedness of the global economy, the risks of financial deregulation, and the need for international cooperation in addressing economic challenges.

7. **Climate Change:** The recognition of climate change as a global crisis has led to a shift in the current global situation. The Paris Agreement, signed in 2015, marked a significant milestone in international efforts to address climate change. The agreement has prompted countries to take actions to mitigate greenhouse gas emissions, adapt to the

impacts of climate change, and transition to a low-carbon economy. Climate change has become a key factor in shaping global politics, security, and economic policies.

8. **Technological Advancements:** Rapid advancements in technology, particularly in the fields of information technology, artificial intelligence, and biotechnology, have transformed the current global situation. The advancements in information technology have revolutionized communication, connectivity, and access to information. The rise of social media platforms has facilitated the spread of information, the mobilization of social and political movements, and the emergence of new forms of digital diplomacy. Artificial intelligence has the potential to reshape industries, automate processes, and enhance military capabilities. Additionally, biotechnology advancements have contributed to breakthroughs in healthcare, agriculture, and environmental conservation.

9. **Global Terrorism:** The rise of global terrorism, particularly the attacks of September 11, 2001, has

had a profound impact on the current global situation. These events led to significant shifts in national security policies, the reevaluation of counterterrorism strategies, and the emergence of new forms of cooperation and intelligence sharing among nations. The fight against terrorism has influenced domestic politics, international relations, and the perception of security threats worldwide.

10. **Pandemics:** The outbreak of pandemics, such as the ongoing COVID-19 pandemic, has had a transformative impact on the current global situation. The rapid spread of infectious diseases has highlighted the interconnectedness of the world and the need for global cooperation in addressing public health crises. The pandemic has disrupted economies, strained healthcare systems, and led to changes in social behavior and international travel. It has also emphasized the importance of scientific collaboration, preparedness, and resilience in the face of future health emergencies.

11. **Multilateral Institutions:** International organizations and multilateral institutions, such as

the United Nations, World Trade Organization, International Monetary Fund, and World Health Organization, have played a crucial role in shaping the current global situation. These institutions provide platforms for global dialogue, cooperation, and the resolution of conflicts. They establish norms, rules, and regulations that govern international relations and address global challenges. However, their effectiveness and relevance have been questioned, leading to debates about reform and the need for more inclusive and representative global governance.

The current global situation is the result of complex interactions among these key players and events. Their actions and decisions have shaped the geopolitical landscape, influenced economic systems, affected social dynamics, and defined the priorities and challenges of the international community. Understanding the roles of these players and events is essential for comprehending the intricacies of global affairs and developing strategies to address the pressing issues of our time.

Technological advancements, particularly in information technology, have transformed the current global situation by revolutionizing communication, connectivity, and access to information. The rise of the internet and social media platforms has fundamentally altered how people interact, share information, and mobilize social and political movements. Social media platforms have provided a space for individuals and groups to express their opinions, raise awareness about social issues, and organize collective action. They have played a significant role in shaping political landscapes, influencing public opinion, and even facilitating political change in some cases.

Moreover, information technology has given rise to new forms of digital diplomacy, where governments and international organizations utilize digital platforms to engage with foreign populations, promote their policies, and influence public opinion. Digital diplomacy enables real-time communication, enables the rapid dissemination of information, and allows for direct engagement with global audiences. It has expanded the reach and scope of traditional diplomacy, presenting both opportunities and challenges for international relations.

Artificial intelligence (AI) is another technological advancement that has the potential to reshape industries, automate processes, and enhance military capabilities. AI technologies, such as machine learning and robotics, have applications in various sectors, including healthcare, transportation, finance, and defense. AI-powered systems have the ability to analyze vast amounts of data, identify patterns, and make predictions, thereby improving decision-making processes and efficiency. However, the rapid development of AI also raises ethical concerns, such as privacy, bias, and the impact on employment.

The current global situation has been shaped by a combination of key players and events, including technological advancements, the rise of global terrorism, pandemics, and the role of multilateral institutions. These factors have influenced the geopolitical landscape, economic systems, social dynamics, and security priorities on a global scale. The interplay between these key players and events has resulted in a complex and interconnected web of relationships, challenges, and opportunities that define the current global situation.

Summary

The history of nuclear politics spans several decades and is marked by significant milestones, including the development, proliferation, and control of nuclear weapons. It encompasses key events, treaties, and policy decisions that have shaped the global nuclear landscape. Understanding the history of nuclear politics is crucial for informing current discussions and actions related to nuclear disarmament, non-proliferation, and arms control.

Action Points

1. **Learn from historical lessons:** Study and analyze the historical events and decisions in nuclear politics to draw lessons and insights that can inform present and future actions. Understand the consequences of past policies, conflicts, and arms races to make more informed choices in contemporary nuclear politics.
2. **Strengthen arms control and non-proliferation regimes:** Build upon the successes and shortcomings of historical arms control and non-

proliferation treaties, such as the Treaty on the Non-Proliferation of Nuclear Weapons (NPT), to strengthen and update existing regimes. Seek innovative approaches to enhance verification mechanisms, promote compliance, and address emerging challenges in nuclear proliferation.

3. **Promote transparency and trust-building measures:** Emphasize the importance of transparency and confidence-building measures in nuclear politics. Encourage states to voluntarily provide information, exchange data, and engage in cooperative efforts to build trust and reduce the risks of miscalculations and misunderstandings.

4. **Foster dialogue and diplomatic engagement:** Prioritize diplomatic dialogue and engagement among nuclear-armed and non-nuclear-armed states to address historical grievances, resolve disputes, and build mutual understanding. Foster a culture of open communication, negotiation, and collaboration to navigate the complexities of nuclear politics.

5. **Educate and raise public awareness:** Promote public education and awareness on the history of

nuclear politics to foster informed public discourse and engagement. Increase public understanding of the risks, consequences, and policy choices associated with nuclear weapons, encouraging active participation in discussions on disarmament, non-proliferation, and peaceful uses of nuclear energy.

Chapter 2

Nuclear Deterrence

Concept of Nuclear Deterrence

Nuclear deterrence is a concept in international relations that refers to the use of nuclear weapons as a means of preventing an adversary from taking aggressive action against a state. The basic idea behind nuclear deterrence is that if a state possesses nuclear weapons, it can deter its adversaries from launching an attack because the consequences of such an attack would be too severe.

The concept of nuclear deterrence emerged during the Cold War, when the United States and the Soviet Union were engaged in a nuclear arms race. The two superpowers built up massive nuclear arsenals in order to deter each other from launching a first strike. The logic was that if one side were to attack the other with nuclear weapons, the response would be so devastating that neither side would want to risk it.

Nuclear deterrence relies on the principle of *mutually assured destruction (MAD),* which holds that if two states possess enough nuclear weapons to destroy each other, they will be deterred from launching an attack. This is because the consequences of a nuclear war would be so catastrophic that neither side would want to risk it.

There are two main types of nuclear deterrence: *direct deterrence* and *extended deterrence*.

Direct deterrence refers to the use of nuclear weapons to deter a direct attack on a state's own territory.

Extended deterrence, on the other hand, refers to the use of nuclear weapons to deter an attack on an ally or partner state.

The effectiveness of nuclear deterrence depends on several factors. First and foremost, it depends on the credibility of a state's nuclear arsenal. If an adversary does not believe that a state would be willing to use nuclear weapons in response to an attack, then nuclear deterrence will not be effective. This is why states invest heavily in developing and maintaining their nuclear arsenals, as well as in demonstrating their willingness to use them if necessary.

Another factor that affects the effectiveness of nuclear deterrence is the degree of uncertainty surrounding a state's nuclear capabilities and intentions. If an adversary is uncertain about a state's nuclear capabilities or intentions, then nuclear deterrence may not be effective.

This is why transparency and communication are important in nuclear deterrence. States must be able to communicate clearly and openly about their nuclear capabilities and intentions in order to avoid misunderstandings and miscalculations.

The concept of nuclear deterrence has been the subject of much debate and criticism over the years. Critics argue that nuclear deterrence is inherently unstable and that the risk of accidental nuclear war is too great. They also argue that nuclear deterrence creates a security dilemma in which states are forced to continually build up their nuclear arsenals in order to maintain their deterrence posture, which in turn fuels further arms races and tensions. Proponents of nuclear deterrence, on the other hand, argue that it has been effective in preventing major wars between nuclear-armed states. They point to the fact that the United States and the Soviet Union were able to avoid a direct military confrontation during the Cold War, despite numerous crises and close calls.

In recent years, the concept of nuclear deterrence has faced new challenges, such as the proliferation of nuclear weapons to new states and the emergence of new threats such as cyberattacks and terrorism. These challenges have led to renewed debate about the effectiveness and stability of nuclear deterrence in the 21st century.

Nuclear deterrence is a concept that has played a significant role in shaping the international security environment over the past several decades. While it has been effective in preventing major wars between nuclear-armed states, it is not without its critics and challenges. As the world continues to grapple with the risks and challenges of nuclear weapons, the concept of nuclear deterrence is likely to remain a central issue in international security.

Strengths and Weaknesses of this Strategy

Nuclear deterrence as a strategy has both strengths and weaknesses. Understanding these strengths and weaknesses is crucial for assessing the effectiveness and potential risks associated with relying on nuclear weapons for deterrence.

Strengths of Nuclear Deterrence:

1. Prevention of Major Wars: One of the primary strengths of nuclear deterrence is its perceived effectiveness in preventing major wars between nuclear-armed states. The fear of *mutually assured destruction (MAD)* and the catastrophic consequences of a nuclear exchange provide strong incentives for states to avoid direct military confrontations. This has been evident during the Cold War, where the presence of nuclear weapons is believed to have contributed to strategic stability and prevented large-scale conflict between the United States and the Soviet Union.

The prevention of major wars is indeed one of the primary strengths of nuclear deterrence. During the Cold War, the United States and the Soviet Union found themselves in a state of intense rivalry and ideological conflict. However, the presence of nuclear weapons on both sides acted as a powerful deterrent against direct military confrontation.

The concept of *mutually assured destruction (MAD)* played a significant role in shaping the dynamics of the Cold War. **MAD** suggests that if two nuclear-armed adversaries engage in a full-scale war, the outcome would be so catastrophic that it would result in the complete annihilation of both sides. The destructive power of nuclear weapons, combined with the potential for massive civilian casualties and long-lasting environmental consequences, created a strong disincentive for engaging in all-out warfare.

The fear of mutual destruction created a delicate balance of power between the United States and the Soviet Union, leading to what was often referred to as "balance of terror." Both sides recognized that launching a nuclear attack would result in devastating retaliation, ensuring that neither side had a decisive advantage. This balance of power contributed to strategic stability, as neither side could risk initiating a conflict that could escalate to a nuclear exchange.

The concept of nuclear deterrence relied on the credibility of a state's nuclear capabilities and its willingness to use them in response to an attack. This credibility was based on the notion of maintaining a secure second-strike capability. In other words, even if one side were to launch a surprise attack, the other side's survivable nuclear forces would be able to retaliate and cause unacceptable damage. This ensured that both sides had a strong incentive to avoid initiating a conflict that could potentially lead to a devastating nuclear war.

Throughout the Cold War, there were several instances

where nuclear deterrence played a role in preventing major wars. The Cuban Missile Crisis in 1962 is a notable example. The United States and the Soviet Union came dangerously close to direct military confrontation when the Soviet Union deployed nuclear missiles in Cuba. However, both sides recognized the risks involved and ultimately reached a negotiated settlement to de-escalate the situation, avoiding a potentially catastrophic conflict.

The experience of the Cold War has shaped the perception of nuclear deterrence as an effective strategy in preventing major wars. The absence of a direct military conflict between the United States and the Soviet Union during this period is often attributed to the deterrence provided by their respective nuclear arsenals. This has influenced the understanding of nuclear deterrence as a stabilizing force in international relations.

However, it is important to note that the prevention of major wars through nuclear deterrence is not without its risks and uncertainties. The reliance on nuclear weapons for deterrence carries the potential for accidental escalation, miscalculation, or the emergence of non-state actors who may not be susceptible to traditional deterrence calculations. The evolving nature of the international security landscape, with the emergence of new nuclear-armed states and the potential for emerging technologies, adds complexity to the effectiveness of nuclear deterrence in preventing major wars.

Overall, while the prevention of major wars is considered a strength of nuclear deterrence, it is essential to continue evaluating the risks, challenges, and evolving dynamics associated with this strategy. Continued efforts to promote disarmament, nonproliferation, and arms control can contribute to maintaining and enhancing the stability provided by nuclear deterrence while reducing the risks associated with the existence of nuclear weapons.

2. Security Assurance: Nuclear weapons can provide a sense of security and assurance for states that possess them. The possession of a credible nuclear arsenal can deter potential aggressors from attacking, as the risk of massive retaliation is a significant deterrent. This perceived security can contribute to a state's strategic stability and enhance its overall national security.

The concept of security assurance is an important strength

of nuclear deterrence. States that possess nuclear weapons believe that their possession provides a sense of security and serves as a deterrent against potential aggressors. The underlying principle is that the risk of a devastating nuclear retaliation acts as a deterrent, dissuading other states from launching an attack.

The possession of a credible nuclear arsenal creates a perception of strength and capability. It signals to potential adversaries that any hostile action or aggression would result in severe consequences. This perception of assured retaliation plays a crucial role in shaping the behavior of other states and discourages them from engaging in acts that could lead to conflict.

The idea of security assurance through nuclear deterrence is based on the principle of deterrence theory, which posits that the threat of severe punishment or retaliation can prevent an adversary from taking action. In the context of nuclear weapons, the potential consequences of a nuclear exchange are so catastrophic that states are inclined to avoid initiating a conflict.

The possession of nuclear weapons can enhance a state's overall national security. It creates a strategic environment in which potential adversaries must consider the risk and consequences of engaging in aggressive actions. This can contribute to a state's deterrence posture and serve as a deterrent against conventional attacks as well. The fear of crossing the nuclear threshold acts as a restraint on potential aggressors, as they weigh the potential costs and risks associated with an attack.

The security assurance provided by nuclear weapons can be particularly relevant for states that perceive themselves as vulnerable to external threats. For states with smaller populations, limited conventional military capabilities, or located in volatile regions, the possession of nuclear weapons can serve as a critical equalizer. It provides them with a means to deter potential aggression from larger or more powerful adversaries.

Additionally, nuclear deterrence can contribute to strategic stability by establishing a balance of power among nuclear-armed states. The possession of nuclear weapons by multiple states creates a situation where no single state can achieve absolute military superiority. This balance of power reduces the likelihood of a pre-emptive strike or an offensive action, as the risks and consequences are seen as too high.

However, it is important to acknowledge that security assurance through nuclear deterrence is not foolproof and comes with its limitations and risks. First, it assumes rational decision-making by all actors involved. The effectiveness of nuclear deterrence relies on the assumption that potential adversaries will act in a predictable and rational manner. However, uncertainties, misperceptions, or the emergence of non-state actors may challenge this assumption.

Second, the possession of nuclear weapons does not guarantee security against all types of threats. Nuclear deterrence primarily focuses on deterring nuclear attacks, and it may not be effective against non-nuclear threats, such as terrorism or cyberattacks. Therefore, states must complement their nuclear deterrence strategies with other forms of security measures to address a wide range of potential threats.

Furthermore, the reliance on nuclear weapons for security assurance perpetuates a reliance on a destructive and potentially catastrophic means of deterrence. It does not address the underlying causes of conflict or promote lasting peace. The pursuit of disarmament, nonproliferation, and arms control remains crucial in mitigating the risks associated with nuclear weapons and promoting a more secure and stable world.

The concept of security assurance is a key strength of nuclear deterrence. The possession of a credible nuclear arsenal can serve as a deterrent, dissuading potential aggressors from launching attacks. It creates a perception of strength and capability, enhances a state's overall national security, and contributes to strategic stability. However, it is essential to recognize the limitations and risks associated with nuclear deterrence and to continue working towards disarmament and nonproliferation efforts for long-term peace and security.

3. Strategic Stability: Nuclear deterrence can contribute to strategic stability by maintaining a balance of power between nuclear-armed states. The existence of nuclear weapons forces states to carefully consider the consequences of their actions, leading to a certain level of predictability in the international system. This predictability can help prevent accidental escalation and reduce the likelihood of miscalculation by adversaries. Strategic stability is a key strength of nuclear deterrence.

It refers to a state of affairs in which the risk of a nuclear war is minimized, and there is a balance of power among nuclear-armed states that discourages aggressive actions. Nuclear deterrence contributes to strategic stability by creating a predictable and cautious environment in which states carefully consider the potential consequences of their actions.

The existence of nuclear weapons compels states to engage in careful strategic calculations and risk assessments. The destructive power of nuclear weapons and the potential for massive retaliation create a strong incentive for states to avoid actions that could escalate into a nuclear conflict. This leads to a level of predictability in the decision-making processes of nuclear-armed states, as they weigh the risks and consequences of their actions.

Nuclear deterrence can help prevent accidental escalation and reduce the likelihood of miscalculation. The high stakes involved in a nuclear conflict and the catastrophic consequences of a nuclear exchange create a strong incentive for caution and restraint. The fear of triggering a nuclear war encourages states to establish communication channels, engage in crisis management mechanisms, and adopt measures to reduce the risks of accidental or unauthorized use of nuclear weapons.

Moreover, the possession of a credible nuclear arsenal by multiple states creates a balance of power that promotes caution and restraint. The concept of mutual deterrence, often referred to as the doctrine of *mutually assured destruction (MAD)*, rests on the notion that both sides possess sufficient retaliatory capabilities to inflict unacceptable damage on each other. This balance of power reduces the incentives for a first-strike attack, as the risks and costs of initiating a nuclear conflict are deemed too high.

The predictability and caution associated with nuclear deterrence contribute to strategic stability by providing a framework for managing international relations. Adversaries in a nuclear-armed environment are more likely to seek diplomatic solutions, engage in arms control negotiations, and pursue confidence-building measures. This can help establish norms of behavior, promote dialogue, and reduce tensions between nuclear-armed states.

However, it is important to recognize that strategic stability is not absolute and can be affected by various factors. Technological advancements, shifts in political dynamics, and changes in the international security environment can introduce uncertainties and challenges to strategic stability. For example, the emergence of new nuclear-armed states or the development of advanced missile defense systems can disrupt the balance of power and create incentives for arms races or destabilizing behaviors.

Furthermore, the stability provided by nuclear deterrence can sometimes lead to complacency or a false sense of security. It is essential for states to continue investing in diplomatic efforts, arms control agreements, and confidence-building measures to reinforce strategic stability and prevent unintended escalations.

Strategic stability is a strength of nuclear deterrence. It promotes predictability, discourages aggressive actions, and reduces the likelihood of miscalculation or accidental escalation. By establishing a balance of power and encouraging cautious decision-making, nuclear deterrence contributes to a relatively stable international system. However, it is important to continuously adapt to changing circumstances and actively pursue diplomatic efforts to reinforce and strengthen strategic stability.

4. Nonproliferation Incentives: Nuclear deterrence can act as an incentive for non-nuclear-armed states to refrain from seeking nuclear weapons. The fear of provoking a nuclear-armed adversary's response or the concern of triggering an arms race can discourage states from pursuing their own nuclear programs. The existence of nuclear deterrence can thus contribute to nonproliferation efforts by discouraging additional states from acquiring nuclear weapons.

Nonproliferation incentives are indeed a significant strength of nuclear deterrence. The fear of provoking a nuclear-armed adversary's response and the concerns of triggering an arms race can act as powerful deterrents for non-nuclear-armed states considering the acquisition of nuclear weapons.

States without nuclear weapons often perceive the possession of nuclear weapons by other states as a significant security challenge. The concept of nuclear deterrence, with its underlying principle of *mutually assured destruction (MAD)*, creates a strong disincentive for non-nuclear-armed states to pursue nuclear weapons.

They are aware that acquiring nuclear capabilities would likely invite severe repercussions from existing nuclear-armed states. The risk of a devastating response and the fear of escalating conflict provide a powerful deterrent against the pursuit of nuclear weapons.

Moreover, the existence of nuclear deterrence can contribute to a broader normative framework that discourages the proliferation of nuclear weapons. International norms and nonproliferation treaties, such as the Treaty on the *Non-Proliferation of Nuclear Weapons (NPT)*, aim to prevent the spread of nuclear weapons and promote disarmament. Nuclear deterrence reinforces these norms by highlighting the risks and dangers associated with nuclear proliferation. It underscores the view that possessing nuclear weapons is not only costly and risky but also unnecessary for the security of non-nuclear-armed states.

Nuclear deterrence also affects the calculations of non-nuclear-armed states by influencing their perception of their own security needs. Rather than investing in costly and potentially destabilizing nuclear programs, non-nuclear-armed states may opt for alternative security strategies. These strategies often involve relying on alliances, regional security arrangements, and diplomatic engagement to ensure their security. By demonstrating that security can be achieved without resorting to nuclear weapons, nuclear deterrence acts as a positive incentive for nonproliferation efforts.

Additionally, the international community, including nuclear-armed states, often emphasizes the importance of nonproliferation and actively works to dissuade states from acquiring nuclear weapons. Diplomatic efforts, economic sanctions, and political pressure can be applied to discourage and prevent non-nuclear-armed states from pursuing nuclear programs. The existence of nuclear deterrence strengthens the credibility of these efforts by demonstrating the severe consequences of nuclear proliferation.

However, it is important to note that nuclear deterrence alone cannot completely eliminate the risk of nuclear proliferation. Non-nuclear-armed states may still have their own unique security concerns, regional dynamics, or domestic political factors that influence their decisions regarding nuclear weapons. In some cases, the pursuit of nuclear weapons may be driven by perceptions of insecurity or as a means to enhance their status and influence on the global stage.

Additionally, the effectiveness of nuclear deterrence as a nonproliferation incentive may vary depending on the specific regional or geopolitical context. Factors such as the presence of regional rivalries, ongoing conflicts, or perceptions of nuclear-armed adversaries' behavior can complicate the decision-making process for non-nuclear-armed states.

Nuclear deterrence can act as a strong incentive for non-nuclear-armed states to refrain from acquiring nuclear weapons. The fear of provoking a nuclear-armed adversary's response and the concerns of triggering an arms race provide powerful deterrents. By reinforcing nonproliferation norms and highlighting alternative security strategies, nuclear deterrence contributes to global efforts to prevent the spread of nuclear weapons. However, it is crucial to continue diplomatic efforts, arms control agreements, and regional security initiatives to strengthen nonproliferation regimes and address the underlying security concerns that may drive states towards nuclear proliferation.

Weaknesses of Nuclear Deterrence:

1. **Risk of Accidental Nuclear War:** The reliance on nuclear deterrence carries inherent risks, including the potential for accidental nuclear war. Factors such as miscommunication, technical malfunctions, false alarms, or cyberattacks can lead to unintended nuclear escalation. These risks increase as the number of nuclear-armed states and non-state actors expands, making the possibility of accidental nuclear conflict a growing concern.

2. **Proliferation Challenges:** While nuclear deterrence can discourage some states from pursuing nuclear weapons, it does not completely eliminate the risk of proliferation. The possession of nuclear weapons by some states may incentivize others to seek their own nuclear capabilities for security reasons or to counterbalance perceived threats. This can lead to regional arms races and increase the likelihood of nuclear proliferation.

3. **Limited Effectiveness against Non-state Actors:** Nuclear deterrence is primarily designed to deter

state actors. It is less effective in deterring non-state actors, such as terrorist groups, which may not be susceptible to the same calculations of mutual destruction. Non-state actors may be willing to engage in acts of terrorism or asymmetric warfare, disregarding the conventional rules of deterrence.

4. **Ethical and Humanitarian Concerns:** The use of nuclear weapons carries significant ethical and humanitarian concerns. The catastrophic humanitarian consequences resulting from a nuclear exchange, including massive loss of life, long-term environmental damage, and radiation effects, raise questions about the morality of relying on weapons with such destructive power as a means of deterrence. The potential indiscriminate and uncontrollable nature of nuclear weapons is a source of ethical debate.

5. **Arms Race Tendencies:** Nuclear deterrence can contribute to arms race dynamics. The perceived need to maintain a credible nuclear deterrent can lead states to continuously modernize and expand their nuclear arsenals, increasing the risks of proliferation and exacerbating global tensions. The

potential for arms races can strain national economies, divert resources from other pressing social needs, and heighten the overall risks of conflict.

Nuclear deterrence has strengths in preventing major wars, providing security assurance, maintaining strategic stability, and encouraging nonproliferation. However, it also carries weaknesses such as the risk of accidental nuclear war, proliferation challenges, limited effectiveness against non-state actors, ethical concerns, and the potential for arms races. Evaluating these strengths and weaknesses is crucial for informed discussions on the role and future of nuclear deterrence in international security.

Examples of Successful and Unsuccessful Deterrence

Successful and unsuccessful deterrence efforts have shaped the course of international relations and have had profound implications for global security. Examining specific examples of both successful and unsuccessful deterrence can provide insights into the dynamics, strategies, and outcomes of deterrence efforts.

Examples of Successful Deterrence:

1. Cold War Deterrence: The Cold War between the United States and the Soviet Union is often cited as a successful example of deterrence. The possession of large nuclear arsenals by both superpowers created a state of mutually assured destruction (MAD), where the fear of catastrophic retaliation acted as a strong deterrent against direct military conflict. Despite numerous proxy wars and confrontations, the fear of escalation to a full-scale nuclear war prevented a direct confrontation between the United States and the Soviet Union.

The Cold War period from the late 1940s to the early 1990s was characterized by intense rivalry and ideological differences between the United States and the Soviet Union. Both nations emerged as superpowers with significant military capabilities, including the development of large nuclear arsenals. The concept of deterrence played a central role in maintaining a fragile peace between the two adversaries.

One of the key factors contributing to the success of deterrence during the Cold War was the doctrine of *mutually assured destruction (MAD)*. MAD postulated that any use of nuclear weapons would result in the annihilation of both sides, leading to a stalemate where neither side could emerge as a clear victor. This understanding created a strong disincentive for direct military confrontation between the United States and the Soviet Union.

The possession of large nuclear arsenals by both superpowers acted as a significant deterrent. The sheer destructive power and potential consequences of a nuclear exchange ensured that both sides exercised caution and restraint. This fear of catastrophic retaliation provided a strong incentive to pursue diplomatic solutions and engage in arms control negotiations rather than risking all-out war.

Furthermore, the development of sophisticated surveillance and early warning systems played a crucial role in maintaining stability. These systems allowed both sides to monitor each other's military activities and detect potential threats. The knowledge that any aggressive action would be quickly detected and could trigger an immediate response further reinforced the deterrence effect.

Another contributing factor to the success of Cold War deterrence was the establishment of direct communication channels between the United States and the Soviet Union. The establishment of the "hotline" in 1963, a direct link between the leaders of both nations, enabled rapid and direct communication in times of crisis. This direct communication channel helped to reduce the risk of misunderstandings, misinterpretations, and miscalculations that could lead to unintended escalation.

Additionally, arms control agreements and treaties, such as the *Strategic Arms Limitation Talks (SALT)* and the *Intermediate-Range Nuclear Forces (INF) Treaty*, provided a framework for managing and reducing the nuclear arms race. These agreements aimed to limit the deployment and proliferation of certain categories of nuclear weapons and established verification mechanisms to ensure compliance. While not eliminating nuclear weapons entirely, these agreements contributed to stability by imposing constraints and increasing transparency.

Despite the numerous proxy conflicts and confrontations that occurred during the Cold War, such as the Korean War, Vietnam War, and various regional conflicts, direct military confrontation between the United States and the Soviet Union was successfully deterred. Both sides understood the catastrophic consequences of a nuclear war and the potential for escalation beyond their control. As a result, the Cold War ended without a direct military conflict between the two superpowers.

However, it is important to acknowledge that the success of Cold War deterrence was not without its flaws and risks. The world lived in a state of constant tension, and the potential for accidental nuclear war or miscalculations remained a persistent concern. The Cuban Missile Crisis in 1962 highlighted the inherent dangers and close calls that could arise despite the presence of deterrence. It took careful diplomacy and negotiation to resolve the crisis and avoid a catastrophic outcome.

Furthermore, the success of deterrence during the Cold War was contingent on the rational behavior of both superpowers and their commitment to avoiding nuclear conflict. It relied on a shared understanding of the devastating consequences of nuclear war and the willingness to exercise restraint. The dynamics of deterrence may not apply uniformly to all states or in all situations, as demonstrated by examples of unsuccessful deterrence efforts in subsequent years.

The Cold War between the United States and the Soviet Union stands as a notable example of successful deterrence. The possession of large nuclear arsenals, the doctrine of mutually assured destruction, robust surveillance systems, direct communication channels, and arms control agreements collectively contributed to maintaining stability and preventing a direct military confrontation. However, the success of Cold War deterrence should not overshadow the ongoing need for continued efforts to promote disarmament, arms control, and diplomatic solutions to prevent future conflicts and reduce the risks associated with nuclear weapons.

2. Indo-Pakistani Deterrence: The nuclear deterrence between India and Pakistan has been relatively successful in preventing a large-scale conflict between the two nuclear-armed neighbors. Both countries possess nuclear weapons, and the fear of massive retaliation has played a significant role in preventing major military escalations. While there have been smaller-scale conflicts and skirmishes between India and Pakistan, the presence of nuclear weapons has contributed to restraint and a focus on diplomatic solutions.

The Indo-Pakistani deterrence relationship is often cited as a case of successful deterrence due to the role nuclear weapons have played in preventing large-scale conflicts between the two countries. India and Pakistan, both possessing nuclear capabilities, have engaged in several military confrontations and border skirmishes since their independence in 1947. However, the introduction of nuclear weapons has significantly influenced the dynamics between the two nations and acted as a restraining factor.

One of the key strengths of nuclear deterrence in the Indo-Pakistani context is the fear of massive retaliation. Both countries possess a credible nuclear deterrent, and the understanding that any large-scale military aggression could trigger a devastating nuclear response has provided a strong incentive for restraint. The concept of mutually assured destruction (MAD) is believed to have influenced the strategic thinking of decision-makers in both countries, dissuading them from engaging in direct military conflicts that could escalate to the nuclear level.

The presence of nuclear weapons has also contributed to a heightened sense of caution and a focus on diplomatic solutions. The potential consequences of a nuclear conflict have forced India and Pakistan to seek diplomatic channels and engage in negotiations to manage their disputes. International pressure and mediation efforts have also played a role in encouraging dialogue and preventing escalations. Examples of crisis management and confidence-building measures, such as the Lahore Declaration in 1999 and the bilateral ceasefire agreement in 2003, have showcased the importance of diplomatic engagement in defusing tensions and preventing further conflict.

Moreover, the existence of nuclear deterrence has led to stability in certain areas. The Line of Control (LoC) in

Kashmir, for instance, has seen a relatively stable military situation due to the recognition of the risks associated with escalating tensions. Both India and Pakistan understand that the use of nuclear weapons in such a contested region would have dire consequences for both sides, leading to a cautious approach and limited military engagements.

However, it is important to note that while nuclear deterrence has been effective in preventing a large-scale conflict, it has not eliminated all forms of hostility between India and Pakistan. There have been instances of low-intensity conflicts and border skirmishes, particularly in the disputed region of Kashmir. These conflicts have resulted in casualties and increased tensions between the two countries. Nevertheless, the presence of nuclear weapons has acted as a restraint, preventing these conflicts from escalating to an all-out war.

Additionally, the stability provided by nuclear deterrence in the Indo-Pakistani context is not without its challenges and risks. The potential for accidental nuclear escalation or unauthorized use of nuclear weapons remains a concern. The lack of robust communication and crisis management mechanisms between India and Pakistan has heightened the risks of miscommunication and misperception, which could potentially lead to unintended consequences. Efforts to enhance communication channels and establish nuclear risk reduction measures have been limited but are necessary to further strengthen deterrence stability.

The nuclear deterrence between India and Pakistan has been relatively successful in preventing large-scale conflicts between the two countries. The fear of massive retaliation and the recognition of the catastrophic consequences of a nuclear exchange have acted as a significant deterrent. While smaller conflicts and border skirmishes have occurred, the presence of nuclear weapons has contributed to restraint and a focus on diplomatic solutions. However, ongoing efforts to improve communication, crisis management, and confidence-building measures are essential to further enhance stability and reduce the risks associated with nuclear weapons in the region.

3. Israeli Nuclear Deterrence: Israel's policy of nuclear ambiguity, neither confirming nor denying its possession of nuclear weapons, has been regarded as a successful deterrence strategy. The perceived nuclear capabilities of Israel have deterred potential adversaries from launching full-scale military actions against the country. Israel's policy of deliberate ambiguity has created uncertainty and added to the deterrent effect of its presumed nuclear capabilities.

Israel's nuclear deterrence strategy, often referred to as the policy of nuclear ambiguity or opacity, has been seen as a successful deterrent against potential adversaries in the region. While Israel has never officially acknowledged or confirmed its possession of nuclear weapons, it is widely believed to have a nuclear arsenal. This deliberate ambiguity surrounding its nuclear capabilities has played a significant role in shaping the strategic dynamics in the Middle East.

One of the primary strengths of Israel's policy of nuclear ambiguity is the uncertainty it creates. By neither confirming nor denying its possession of nuclear weapons, Israel has managed to keep its adversaries guessing about its actual capabilities and intentions. This uncertainty adds to the deterrence effect as potential adversaries are cautious and hesitant to launch full-scale military actions against Israel, fearing a disproportionate and devastating response.

The perceived nuclear capabilities of Israel act as a deterrent against potential threats from both state and non-state actors in the region. Israel faces security challenges from various sources, including neighboring countries and non-state actors like terrorist organizations. The ambiguity surrounding its nuclear arsenal serves as a deterrent by raising the costs and risks associated with any hostile actions directed towards Israel. The fear of a nuclear response has contributed to a certain level of strategic stability and deterred adversaries from engaging in large-scale military confrontations.

Furthermore, Israel's policy of nuclear ambiguity has served as a tool for strategic signaling. The calculated ambiguity surrounding its nuclear capabilities allows Israel to send implicit messages to its adversaries, warning them of the potential consequences of aggressive actions. By keeping its adversaries uncertain about the nature and scale of its nuclear arsenal, Israel can effectively leverage the psychological impact of potential nuclear retaliation, thereby enhancing its deterrence posture.

The success of Israel's nuclear deterrence strategy is also attributed to the perceived credibility of its nuclear capabilities. Despite its policy of ambiguity, Israel has taken measures to demonstrate its capability to develop and deliver nuclear weapons if necessary. Its efforts to develop advanced missile defense systems, such as the Arrow and Iron Dome, alongside its conventional military strength, contribute to the perception of a robust and credible deterrence posture. This combination of defensive and offensive capabilities reinforces the notion that any aggression against Israel could result in severe consequences.

However, it is important to note that Israel's nuclear deterrence strategy is not without its challenges and risks. The ambiguity surrounding its nuclear arsenal raises concerns about the potential for a destabilizing arms race in the region. Other states in the Middle East may feel compelled to acquire their own nuclear weapons as a response to Israel's presumed capabilities, which could lead to increased tensions and a heightened risk of nuclear proliferation.

Moreover, the lack of transparency and public

accountability associated with Israel's nuclear policy raises questions about the broader nonproliferation regime. It has been argued that Israel's policy of nuclear ambiguity undermines the principles of transparency and disarmament advocated by the international community. Calls for Israel to join the *Nuclear Non-Proliferation Treaty (NPT)* and subject its nuclear program to international scrutiny have been ongoing, highlighting the potential shortcomings and challenges of its deterrence strategy.

Israel's policy of nuclear ambiguity has been regarded as a successful deterrence strategy. The perceived nuclear capabilities of Israel, combined with the uncertainty and ambiguity surrounding its nuclear arsenal, have deterred potential adversaries from launching large-scale military actions. The policy has created a level of strategic stability in the region and reinforced Israel's security posture. However, the strategy also presents challenges, including the potential for an arms race and questions regarding nonproliferation norms. Balancing the effectiveness of deterrence with the broader goals of nuclear disarmament and stability in the Middle East remains a complex and ongoing challenge.

Examples of Unsuccessful Deterrence:

1. **Cuban Missile Crisis:** The Cuban Missile Crisis in 1962 is an example of a deterrence effort that came dangerously close to failure. The United States and the Soviet Union were engaged in a tense standoff, with the Soviets deploying nuclear missiles to Cuba. The crisis escalated tensions and brought the two superpowers to the brink of a nuclear war. Although the crisis was eventually resolved diplomatically, it highlighted the risks and limitations of deterrence and the potential for miscalculations and unintended consequences.

2. **Iraqi WMD Deterrence:** In the early 2000s, the United States and its allies based their deterrence strategy on the belief that Iraq possessed weapons of mass destruction (WMD). The rationale was that the fear of a U.S. military response would deter Iraq from using or proliferating these weapons. However, the subsequent invasion of Iraq in 2003 revealed that Iraq did not possess the anticipated WMD stockpiles, calling into question the effectiveness of the deterrence strategy and leading to significant

geopolitical consequences.

3. **Ukrainian Crisis:** The annexation of Crimea by Russia in 2014 and the subsequent conflict in Eastern Ukraine demonstrated the limitations of deterrence in the face of an aggressive actor. Despite Ukraine's non-nuclear status and its reliance on international guarantees for its territorial integrity, Russia's actions were not effectively deterred. This raised questions about the credibility and effectiveness of deterrence measures in the modern era and the challenges posed by hybrid warfare tactics.

It is important to note that the success or failure of deterrence efforts is often subjective and can depend on various factors, including the specific context, the goals and intentions of the parties involved, and the evolving geopolitical dynamics. Deterrence is a complex strategy that requires a delicate balance of credible capabilities, clear communication, and a nuanced understanding of the adversary's motivations and decision-making processes. Examples of successful deterrence, such as the Cold War deterrence between the United States and the Soviet Union,

Indo-Pakistani deterrence, and Israeli nuclear deterrence, demonstrate the potential effectiveness of deterrence in preventing major conflicts. However, examples of unsuccessful deterrence, like the Cuban Missile Crisis in 1962 and the ongoing North Korean nuclear program, highlight the limitations and challenges associated with deterrence strategies.

The Cuban Missile Crisis serves as an example of a critical moment in history where deterrence was tested, and the risk of nuclear conflict was at its peak. During the crisis, the United States discovered that the Soviet Union was deploying nuclear missiles in Cuba, which posed a direct threat to U.S. national security. The United States responded with a naval blockade and a clear message that any attack from Cuba would result in a massive retaliation against the Soviet Union. The crisis eventually de-escalated through diplomatic negotiations, and the Soviet Union agreed to withdraw its missiles from Cuba in exchange for a U.S. commitment not to invade Cuba and to remove its missiles from Turkey.

While the Cuban Missile Crisis is often hailed as a successful example of deterrence, it also highlights the risks and dangers associated with the strategy. The crisis brought the world to the brink of nuclear war, with both the United States and the Soviet Union engaging in a high-stakes game of brinkmanship. The inherent uncertainty and the potential for miscommunication or miscalculation during such crises pose significant challenges to the effectiveness of deterrence. The Cuban Missile Crisis serves as a reminder that deterrence can be a delicate balance, and the potential for unintended escalation and catastrophic consequences is ever-present.

Another example of unsuccessful deterrence is the ongoing nuclear program of North Korea. Despite efforts by the international community, including economic sanctions and diplomatic negotiations, North Korea has continued to pursue the development of nuclear weapons and long-range ballistic missiles. The North Korean regime sees nuclear weapons as a means to ensure its survival and maintain its strategic leverage in the region. Despite diplomatic overtures and attempts to dissuade North Korea from its nuclear ambitions, the deterrence strategy has been ineffective in preventing the country from advancing its nuclear program.

The case of North Korea highlights the challenges associated with deterring a determined and isolated regime that places a high value on nuclear weapons for its own security and survival. The complexity of the situation, including regional dynamics and geopolitical considerations, has made it difficult to find a resolution through traditional deterrence mechanisms. The example of North Korea underscores the need for a comprehensive and multifaceted approach that combines deterrence, diplomacy, and international cooperation to address the proliferation challenges posed by certain states.

While there have been successful instances of deterrence, such as the Cold War deterrence between the United States and the Soviet Union, Indo-Pakistani deterrence, and Israeli nuclear deterrence, there have also been cases where deterrence has faced significant challenges and limitations. The Cuban Missile Crisis and the ongoing North Korean nuclear program highlight the complexities and risks associated with deterrence strategies. These examples emphasize the need for continuous diplomatic efforts, international cooperation, and the exploration of alternative approaches to address the evolving threats in the realm of nuclear weapons and nonproliferation.

Summary

Nuclear deterrence refers to the strategy of maintaining a nuclear arsenal to deter potential adversaries from attacking. It is based on the belief that the possession of nuclear weapons serves as a powerful deterrent against aggression. However, nuclear deterrence is a complex and controversial concept that raises important ethical, strategic, and security concerns. Here is a brief summary and five action points based on the discussion so far:

Action Points

1. **Promote dialogue and understanding:** Encourage open and constructive dialogue among states to enhance mutual understanding of nuclear deterrence policies, including their rationale, limitations, and potential risks. Foster discussions that promote transparency, reduce misperceptions, and address concerns related to nuclear deterrence.

2. **Strengthen arms control and disarmament efforts:** Pursue and strengthen arms control and disarmament measures to reduce the reliance on nuclear weapons for deterrence. Advocate for the

ratification and implementation of international treaties, such as the Treaty on the Prohibition of Nuclear Weapons, to move towards a world free of nuclear weapons.

3. **Invest in conflict prevention and resolution:** Prioritize efforts to prevent conflicts and resolve disputes through diplomatic means. Emphasize the role of diplomacy, mediation, and negotiation in resolving international disputes, reducing tensions, and minimizing the need for reliance on nuclear deterrence.

4. **Promote regional security and cooperation:** Encourage regional security arrangements and cooperation to address regional conflicts and security concerns. Facilitate dialogue and confidence-building measures among states to reduce the perceived need for nuclear deterrence and foster a more stable and secure regional environment.

5. **Strengthen non-proliferation efforts:** Intensify efforts to prevent the proliferation of nuclear weapons and technology. Support comprehensive and effective non-proliferation mechanisms, such as

the Treaty on the Non-Proliferation of Nuclear Weapons (NPT), and work towards universal adherence and robust enforcement to limit the spread of nuclear weapons.

Chapter 3

Disarmament – Efforts to Reduce and Eliminate Nuclear Weapons

Efforts to reduce and eliminate nuclear weapons have been a prominent goal of the international community for several decades. Recognizing the devastating consequences of nuclear weapons and the risks they pose to global security, various initiatives, treaties, and diplomatic negotiations have been undertaken to curb the proliferation of nuclear weapons and work towards their eventual elimination.

Here, we will delve into some of the key efforts and initiatives in this regard.

1. **Non-Proliferation Treaty (NPT):** The NPT, which entered into force in 1970, is one of the cornerstones of nuclear disarmament efforts. It aims to prevent the spread of nuclear weapons, promote disarmament, and facilitate the peaceful use of nuclear energy. Under the treaty, non-nuclear-weapon states commit not to acquire nuclear weapons, while nuclear-weapon states commit to

pursuing disarmament negotiations in good faith. The NPT has played a crucial role in preventing the proliferation of nuclear weapons, with the majority of countries in the world becoming parties to the treaty.

2. **Strategic Arms Reduction Treaties (START):** START treaties have been significant in reducing the number of deployed strategic nuclear weapons between the United States and Russia. The **START I Treaty**, signed in 1991, and its successor, the **START II Treaty**, which was signed in 1993 but not ratified, led to substantial reductions in the nuclear arsenals of both countries. The *New START Treaty*, signed in 2010, further reduced the deployed strategic nuclear weapons of the United States and Russia and established a verification and monitoring framework. These treaties demonstrate successful bilateral efforts to reduce the number of nuclear weapons and enhance strategic stability.

3. **Comprehensive Nuclear-Test-Ban Treaty (CTBT):** The CTBT, adopted by the United Nations General Assembly in 1996, prohibits all

nuclear weapon test explosions. Its entry into force is a crucial step towards curbing the development and modernization of nuclear weapons. The treaty aims to establish a global norm against nuclear testing and provides for a comprehensive verification regime to monitor compliance. While the **CTBT** has not yet entered into force due to some key states not ratifying it, its existence contributes to the global norm against nuclear testing.

4. **Nuclear-Weapon-Free Zones (NWFZs):** NWFZs are regions where states have agreed to prohibit the acquisition, testing, and deployment of nuclear weapons. These zones are established through regional treaties, such as the Treaty of Tlatelolco in Latin America and the Caribbean, the Treaty of Rarotonga in the South Pacific, and the Treaty of Pelindaba in Africa. NWFZs contribute to regional security and confidence-building measures by reducing the presence of nuclear weapons in specific regions and promoting disarmament commitments.

5. **Humanitarian Initiatives and Treaty Prohibitions:** In recent years, there have been

growing humanitarian concerns regarding the catastrophic consequences of the use of nuclear weapons. Several international conferences and initiatives have highlighted the humanitarian impact of nuclear weapons and called for their prohibition. This led to the adoption of the Treaty on the *Prohibition of Nuclear Weapons (TPNW)* in 2017. The **TPNW** prohibits the development, testing, production, acquisition, possession, and use of nuclear weapons and calls for their eventual elimination. While the **TPNW** has not been ratified by all nuclear-weapon states and some of their allies, it represents a significant step towards stigmatizing and delegitimizing nuclear weapons.

6. **Disarmament Dialogue and Nuclear Weapon States' Commitments:** Bilateral and multilateral disarmament dialogues and negotiations between nuclear-weapon states and non-nuclear-weapon states play a crucial role in advancing disarmament efforts. These dialogues aim to build trust, enhance transparency, and explore practical steps towards disarmament. Additionally, nuclear-weapon states

have made commitments and issued policy statements to reduce and eliminate nuclear weapons. For example, the United States and Russia have engaged in ongoing strategic dialogue and negotiations, reaffirming their commitment to nuclear disarmament and exploring measures to further reduce their nuclear arsenals. Other nuclear-weapon states, such as the United Kingdom, France, and China, have also expressed their commitment to disarmament, although progress has been relatively slower compared to the U.S. and Russia.

Furthermore, international organizations and initiatives have played a crucial role in advancing disarmament efforts. The *International Atomic Energy Agency (IAEA)* plays a central role in verifying and monitoring compliance with nuclear non-proliferation agreements. It conducts inspections and safeguards activities to ensure that nuclear materials are used for peaceful purposes. The *Proliferation Security Initiative (PSI)* aims to prevent the illicit trafficking of nuclear materials and technology.

Efforts to reduce and eliminate nuclear weapons face various challenges. One of the primary challenges is the complex security dynamics and geopolitical tensions among states. The possession of nuclear weapons is often seen as a strategic deterrent, leading to reluctance among some states to relinquish their nuclear capabilities due to concerns about their security.

Another challenge is the lack of universal participation and commitment to disarmament efforts. While the majority of states have joined the NPT and support disarmament in principle, there are states that remain outside of the treaty and continue to pursue nuclear weapons. The NPT's effectiveness also relies on the nuclear-weapon states fulfilling their disarmament obligations, which has been a subject of criticism and debate.

Additionally, technical challenges exist in verifying and ensuring compliance with disarmament agreements. The dismantlement and verification of nuclear weapons require complex and expensive processes, as well as robust monitoring mechanisms to ensure transparency and prevent cheating.

Overall, despite the challenges, efforts to reduce and eliminate nuclear weapons remain crucial for global peace and security. The international community continues to work towards strengthening existing treaties, promoting disarmament dialogues, and raising awareness about the humanitarian consequences of nuclear weapons. By fostering a culture of disarmament, building trust among states, and reinforcing multilateral cooperation, progress can be made in achieving a world free from the threat of nuclear weapons.

Non-Proliferation Treaty (NPT)

The *Non-Proliferation Treaty (NPT)* is an international treaty aimed at preventing the spread of nuclear weapons, promoting disarmament, and facilitating the peaceful use of nuclear energy. It is widely considered one of the cornerstone agreements in the field of nuclear non-proliferation and arms control. The NPT has been instrumental in shaping the global nuclear order and establishing norms and obligations for states regarding nuclear weapons.

The NPT was opened for signature in 1968 and entered into force in 1970. It currently has 191 states parties, making it one of the most widely adhered-to treaties in the world. The treaty consists of three pillars or main objectives: non-proliferation, disarmament, and the peaceful use of nuclear energy.

1. Non-Proliferation: The non-proliferation aspect of the NPT aims to prevent the further spread of nuclear weapons. It divides states into two categories: *nuclear-weapon states (NWS)* and *non-nuclear-weapon states (NNWS)*. The NWS are the five countries that possessed nuclear weapons at the time the treaty was signed: <u>the United States, Russia, the United Kingdom, France, and China</u>. These states are recognized as nuclear-weapon states under the NPT.

NNWS, on the other hand, commit not to acquire or develop nuclear weapons. They agree to accept *International Atomic Energy Agency (IAEA)* safeguards on their peaceful nuclear activities to verify that they are not diverting nuclear materials for military purposes. **NNWS** have the right to access and use nuclear technology for peaceful purposes, such as energy production and medical applications.

Under the non-proliferation aspect of the *NPT, non-nuclear-weapon states (NNWS)* commit to refraining from acquiring or developing nuclear weapons. This commitment is reinforced by the acceptance of *International Atomic Energy Agency (IAEA)* safeguards on their peaceful nuclear activities. The purpose of these safeguards is to ensure that nuclear materials and facilities are used exclusively for peaceful purposes and to verify compliance with non-proliferation obligations.

The **IAEA** safeguards system involves monitoring and inspections carried out by the **IAEA** to verify the declared nuclear activities of *NNWS*. These safeguards include measures such as the verification of nuclear material inventories, the monitoring of nuclear facilities, and the analysis of data provided by states. The *IAEA's* objective is to provide assurance to the international community that nuclear materials are not being diverted for military purposes.

By accepting *IAEA* safeguards, *NNWS* demonstrate their commitment to non-proliferation and contribute to the overall stability of the nuclear non-proliferation regime. These safeguards help build confidence among states and ensure that peaceful uses of nuclear energy, such as electricity generation, medical applications, and scientific research, can be pursued without the risk of diversion for military purposes.

Furthermore, the NPT recognizes the inalienable right of NNWS to access and use nuclear technology for peaceful purposes. This includes the transfer of nuclear materials, equipment, and know-how, as well as international cooperation in the field of peaceful nuclear technology. Such cooperation can support the development of nuclear energy programs for electricity generation, nuclear medicine, agriculture, and other peaceful applications.

The non-proliferation aspect of the NPT has contributed to preventing the further spread of nuclear weapons. By committing to non-proliferation obligations and accepting IAEA safeguards, NNWS demonstrate their dedication to peaceful uses of nuclear energy while reinforcing the international norms against the acquisition and development of nuclear weapons.

It is important to note that the non-proliferation aspect of the NPT does not imply a permanent division between nuclear-weapon states (NWS) and non-nuclear-weapon states (NNWS). The treaty recognizes the ultimate goal of achieving nuclear disarmament and calls upon NWS to pursue negotiations in good faith towards disarmament. The differentiation between NWS and NNWS is a temporary measure to maintain strategic stability while progress towards disarmament is pursued.

Overall, the non-proliferation aspect of the NPT establishes a framework that seeks to balance the rights of states to access peaceful nuclear technology with the goal of preventing the proliferation of nuclear weapons. Through IAEA safeguards and international cooperation, NNWS can benefit from the peaceful applications of nuclear energy while contributing to global efforts to prevent the further spread of nuclear weapons.

2. Disarmament: The disarmament aspect of the NPT calls for nuclear-weapon states to pursue negotiations in good faith toward nuclear disarmament. While the NPT recognizes the existing nuclear-weapon states, it aims to achieve their eventual disarmament. This provision reflects the understanding that the ultimate goal of the treaty is the elimination of nuclear weapons.

However, progress in nuclear disarmament has been a subject of ongoing debate and criticism. Some non-nuclear-weapon states argue that the nuclear-weapon states have not fulfilled their disarmament obligations adequately. They call for more concrete and time-bound steps toward disarmament, including further reductions in nuclear arsenals, increased transparency, and the pursuit of a nuclear-weapon-free world.

The disarmament aspect of the *NPT* is a critical pillar that recognizes the goal of achieving nuclear disarmament and calls upon *nuclear-weapon states (NWS)* to engage in negotiations in good faith to pursue disarmament. While the treaty acknowledges the existence of nuclear-weapon states, it emphasizes their eventual disarmament, reflecting the understanding that the long-term objective is the complete elimination of nuclear weapons.

The *NPT* recognizes the inherent tension between non-proliferation and disarmament. On one hand, the non-proliferation aspect aims to prevent the spread of nuclear weapons, while on the other hand, the disarmament aspect aims to reduce and ultimately eliminate existing nuclear arsenals. Achieving a balance between these two objectives is crucial for maintaining the credibility and effectiveness of the treaty.

However, progress in nuclear disarmament has been a subject of ongoing debate and criticism. *Non-nuclear-*

weapon states (NNWS) argue that the pace of disarmament by nuclear-weapon states has been insufficient, and they call for more concrete and time-bound steps toward disarmament. They emphasize the importance of further reductions in nuclear arsenals, increased transparency, and the pursuit of a nuclear-weapon-free world.

One of the challenges in disarmament efforts is the complexity and sensitivity surrounding nuclear weapons. Nuclear-weapon states consider their arsenals as essential for their national security and deterrence strategies. They often cite geopolitical factors, strategic stability concerns, and the need for a step-by-step approach as reasons for the slow progress in disarmament.

To address these concerns, disarmament dialogues and negotiations take place between nuclear-weapon states and non-nuclear-weapon states. These dialogues aim to build trust, enhance transparency, and explore practical steps towards disarmament. The *NPT* Review Conferences, held every five years, provide a platform for states parties to assess the implementation of the treaty's disarmament obligations, discuss challenges, and set future goals.

Efforts have been made to achieve concrete disarmament

measures. Bilateral agreements such as the ***Strategic Arms Reduction Treaties (START)*** between the United States and Russia have resulted in significant reductions in deployed strategic nuclear weapons. The *New START Treaty*, signed in 2010, further reduced the nuclear arsenals of both countries and established a verification and monitoring framework.

In recent years, there have been renewed calls for more ambitious disarmament initiatives. Civil society organizations, international conferences, and initiatives have highlighted the humanitarian impact of nuclear weapons and emphasized the need for their prohibition. This led to the adoption of the *Treaty on the Prohibition of Nuclear Weapons (TPNW)* in 2017, which prohibits the development, testing, production, acquisition, possession, and use of nuclear weapons. The TPNW represents a significant step towards stigmatizing and delegitimizing nuclear weapons, although it has not been ratified by all nuclear-weapon states and some of their allies.

Overall, while progress in nuclear disarmament has faced challenges, efforts continue to be made to fulfill the disarmament obligations of the NPT. Dialogue, transparency, and negotiations between nuclear-weapon states and non-nuclear-weapon states play a vital role in advancing disarmament objectives. The pursuit of further reductions in nuclear arsenals, increased transparency, and the exploration of pathways towards a nuclear-weapon-free world remain key priorities in efforts to reduce and eliminate nuclear weapons.

3. Peaceful Use of Nuclear Energy: The NPT recognizes the right of all parties to the treaty to access and develop nuclear energy for peaceful purposes. It encourages cooperation in the field of nuclear technology and the transfer of peaceful nuclear technology between states parties. However, this cooperation is subject to *IAEA* safeguards to ensure that nuclear materials and technologies are used solely for peaceful purposes.

The *NPT* has been successful in preventing the proliferation of nuclear weapons to a large extent. The vast majority of countries in the world have become parties to the treaty and have committed themselves to forgo nuclear weapons. The treaty's verification regime, implemented by the IAEA, plays a crucial role in monitoring compliance and ensuring the peaceful nature of states' nuclear activities.

The NPT recognizes the right of all parties to access and develop nuclear energy for peaceful purposes. This recognition reflects the understanding that nuclear technology has significant benefits for various peaceful applications, such as electricity generation, medical uses, agriculture, and scientific research. The treaty encourages cooperation among states in the field of nuclear technology, including the transfer of peaceful nuclear technology, to foster peaceful nuclear energy development worldwide.

However, cooperation in the peaceful use of nuclear energy is subject to safeguards implemented by the *International Atomic Energy Agency (IAEA)*. The *IAEA* is responsible for verifying that states' nuclear activities are conducted solely for peaceful purposes and that nuclear materials and technologies are not diverted for military use. Safeguards include inspections, monitoring, and the collection of information to ensure transparency and compliance with treaty obligations.

The *NPT's* provisions regarding the peaceful use of nuclear energy have contributed to the proliferation prevention aspect of the treaty. By allowing states to pursue nuclear energy development for peaceful purposes, the NPT offers an alternative pathway for countries seeking to meet their energy needs without resorting to the acquisition of nuclear weapons. This recognition of the right to access nuclear technology for peaceful purposes has helped to create an environment where countries can benefit from the advantages of nuclear energy while upholding their non-proliferation commitments.

The *NPT's* verification regime, implemented by the *IAEA*, plays a crucial role in monitoring compliance with the treaty's obligations. The IAEA conducts regular inspections and safeguards activities to verify that nuclear facilities and materials are used in accordance with the NPT. The agency's safeguards system acts as a deterrent to potential violators and provides confidence to states that their counterparts are abiding by their non-proliferation commitments.

The success of the NPT in preventing the spread of nuclear weapons can be seen in the high level of participation and adherence to the treaty. The vast majority of countries in the world have become parties to the NPT, signaling their commitment to forgo nuclear weapons and abide by non-proliferation obligations. This widespread adherence to the treaty demonstrates the recognition by states of the value of the NPT as a means to maintain international peace and security.

However, challenges and concerns remain in the peaceful use of nuclear energy. There are ongoing debates regarding the balance between nuclear energy development and non-proliferation efforts. Some critics argue that the peaceful use of nuclear energy can create risks of nuclear weapons proliferation if not properly managed, including the potential diversion of materials or technologies for military purposes. Therefore, it is essential to ensure effective implementation of safeguards and robust international cooperation to promote the safe and secure use of nuclear energy.

The NPT recognizes the right of states to access and develop nuclear energy for peaceful purposes, subject to IAEA safeguards. The treaty's provisions on the peaceful use of nuclear energy have contributed to the prevention of nuclear weapons proliferation. The IAEA's verification regime plays a crucial role in monitoring compliance with non-proliferation obligations. However, ongoing challenges and debates persist regarding the balance between nuclear energy development and non-proliferation efforts, emphasizing the need for continued international cooperation and effective safeguards implementation.

Despite its successes, challenges and criticisms persist regarding the NPT. Some states remain outside the treaty and have pursued or developed nuclear weapons. There are calls for stronger enforcement mechanisms, enhanced verification measures, and greater progress in nuclear disarmament. The NPT Review Conferences, held every five years, provide a forum for states parties to assess the implementation of the treaty, address challenges, and set future goals.

The Non-Proliferation Treaty is a vital international agreement that aims to prevent the spread of nuclear weapons, promote disarmament, and facilitate peaceful nuclear energy use. While significant progress has been made in non-proliferation efforts, further steps are required to address disarmament concerns and strengthen the treaty's effectiveness such as achieving universal adherence, enhancing disarmament commitments, and ensuring the peaceful use of nuclear energy. The NPT remains a cornerstone of the global non-proliferation and disarmament regime and provides a framework for international cooperation and dialogue on nuclear issues.

Recent Treaty on the Prohibition of Nuclear Weapons

The Treaty on the Prohibition of Nuclear Weapons (TPNW) is a recent international treaty that was adopted on July 7, 2017, at the **United Nations (UN)** headquarters in New York. The TPNW represents a significant development in global efforts to eliminate nuclear weapons and has been hailed by its supporters as a crucial step towards a world free of nuclear weapons.

Key Provisions of the Treaty:

1. Prohibition: The TPNW prohibits the development, testing, production, acquisition, possession, stockpiling, transfer, and use of nuclear weapons. It establishes an unequivocal norm against nuclear weapons and aims to delegitimize their possession and use. The treaty considers any assistance or encouragement in these activities as prohibited as well.

The prohibition aspect of the Treaty on the *Prohibition of*

Nuclear Weapons (TPNW) is one of its central and defining features. It establishes a comprehensive and unambiguous ban on nuclear weapons and seeks to delegitimize their possession, use, and other related activities. By prohibiting a range of actions associated with nuclear weapons, the TPNW aims to create a strong norm against these weapons of mass destruction.

The TPNW prohibits the development, testing, production, acquisition, possession, stockpiling, transfer, and use of nuclear weapons. These prohibitions apply to all states parties to the treaty, including both nuclear-weapon states and non-nuclear-weapon states. By encompassing the entire life cycle of nuclear weapons, the treaty aims to leave no room for ambiguity or loopholes in its implementation.

The TPNW's prohibition extends not only to states but also to individuals, groups, and organizations. It considers any assistance, encouragement, or inducement in prohibited activities as prohibited as well. This provision aims to deter and prevent support for the development, possession, or use of nuclear weapons, including financing, technical assistance, or political support.

The treaty's objective is not only to outlaw the possession

and use of nuclear weapons but also to challenge the prevailing perception of nuclear weapons as legitimate instruments of security. It seeks to change the narrative around nuclear weapons and promote the view that these weapons are inherently dangerous and pose an unacceptable threat to humanity.

By establishing a norm against nuclear weapons, the *TPNW* contributes to the broader effort to stigmatize and delegitimize these weapons. The treaty emphasizes the humanitarian consequences of nuclear weapons, highlighting their potential for catastrophic destruction, indiscriminate killing, and long-lasting environmental and health effects.

The *TPNW* builds upon and complements existing disarmament and non-proliferation treaties, such as the Treaty on the *Non-Proliferation of Nuclear Weapons (NPT)*. While the NPT seeks to prevent the spread of nuclear weapons and promotes disarmament, the TPNW takes a more explicit and immediate approach by directly prohibiting nuclear weapons themselves.

It is important to note that the TPNW's prohibition does not automatically result in the elimination of existing nuclear weapons. The treaty does not provide a detailed roadmap for disarmament, and it does not have mechanisms for the verifiable dismantlement of nuclear arsenals. Its focus is primarily on establishing a normative framework and creating political pressure for nuclear disarmament.

The TPNW's prohibition has received support from many non-nuclear-weapon states, civil society organizations, and international humanitarian actors who argue that it represents a necessary step towards a world without nuclear weapons. However, nuclear-weapon states and some of their allies have raised concerns about the treaty's practicality and its potential impact on security dynamics. The prohibition aspect of the Treaty on the Prohibition of Nuclear Weapons establishes a comprehensive and unambiguous ban on nuclear weapons and related activities. It aims to delegitimize the possession, use, and support of nuclear weapons by establishing a strong norm against them. While the treaty's prohibition contributes to the broader effort to eliminate nuclear weapons, its effectiveness in achieving disarmament will depend on the engagement of nuclear-weapon states and broader international support for its objectives.

2. Comprehensive Scope: The TPNW covers all aspects of nuclear weapons, including their use, threat of use, deployment, and stationing of nuclear weapons on the territory of member states. It also encompasses the financing and assistance in prohibited activities related to nuclear weapons.

The Treaty on the Prohibition of Nuclear Weapons (TPNW) has a comprehensive scope that covers all aspects of nuclear weapons, ensuring that the ban extends beyond the mere possession and use of these weapons. The treaty recognizes that the threat posed by nuclear weapons encompasses various dimensions, and it seeks to address them comprehensively.

3. Use and Threat of Use: The TPNW prohibits not only the use of nuclear weapons but also the threat of their use. This prohibition is significant because it recognizes that the mere possession of nuclear weapons creates a constant threat to global peace and security. By including the threat of use, the TPNW aims to discourage nuclear-weapon states from relying on the deterrence value of these weapons and promotes the idea that the use or threat of use of nuclear weapons is unacceptable under any circumstances.

Deployment and Stationing: The treaty also covers the deployment and stationing of nuclear weapons on the territory of member states. It recognizes that the presence of nuclear weapons on a country's soil contributes to the risks and dangers associated with these weapons. The TPNW seeks to prevent states from hosting or allowing the deployment of nuclear weapons on their territories, thereby undermining the perceived legitimacy and normalcy of nuclear weapons possession.

Financing and Assistance: The TPNW goes beyond addressing the actions directly related to nuclear weapons and also covers the financing and assistance in prohibited activities. It recognizes that financial support and assistance provided to states or entities engaged in the development, production, or acquisition of nuclear weapons can contribute to the perpetuation of these weapons. By prohibiting such financing and assistance, the treaty aims to create a disincentive for any form of support that enables the maintenance or expansion of nuclear weapons capabilities.

The comprehensive scope of the TPNW reflects the

understanding that addressing the complex and multifaceted nature of nuclear weapons requires a comprehensive approach. It recognizes that the risks associated with nuclear weapons extend beyond their physical existence and encompass a range of activities and behaviors that contribute to their maintenance and proliferation.

By covering deployment, stationing, and the threat of use, the treaty acknowledges that the mere presence of nuclear weapons and the potential for their use have significant security implications. It challenges the notion that nuclear weapons enhance security and argues that their elimination is essential for ensuring global peace and stability.

Moreover, by prohibiting financing and assistance in prohibited activities, the TPNW seeks to prevent indirect support for nuclear weapons programs. It aims to discourage states, organizations, and individuals from providing resources or assistance that could enable the development or maintenance of nuclear weapons capabilities, reinforcing the norm against these weapons.

The comprehensive scope of the TPNW reinforces its

ambition to address all aspects of nuclear weapons and their impact on global security. By addressing the use, threat of use, deployment, stationing, financing, and assistance related to nuclear weapons, the treaty aims to create a robust and effective framework for the prohibition and elimination of these weapons of mass destruction.

4. Safeguards and Verification: The treaty requires states parties to conclude and implement comprehensive safeguards agreements with the *International Atomic Energy Agency (IAEA)*. These agreements aim to ensure that nuclear materials and facilities are used exclusively for peaceful purposes and to prevent the diversion of such materials for military use.

The Treaty on the *Prohibition of Nuclear Weapons (TPNW)* includes provisions for safeguards and verification to ensure compliance with its obligations. Safeguards are measures implemented by the *International Atomic Energy Agency (IAEA)* to verify that states' nuclear materials and facilities are used exclusively for peaceful purposes and not diverted for military use.

Under the *TPNW*, states parties are required to conclude and implement comprehensive safeguards agreements with the *IAEA*. These agreements are based on the existing

IAEA safeguards system, which is a set of measures designed to detect and deter the diversion of nuclear materials and technology for non-peaceful purposes. The IAEA is responsible for implementing these safeguards and verifying compliance with the TPNW's obligations.

Comprehensive safeguards agreements involve the application of safeguards to all of a state's nuclear activities, including the declaration of nuclear facilities, materials, and related activities. The IAEA conducts regular inspections and monitoring to verify that nuclear materials are accounted for and used exclusively for peaceful purposes. It also assesses the correctness and completeness of states' declarations and investigates any potential indications of undeclared nuclear activities.

The safeguards system includes various measures to ensure the effectiveness and transparency of verification. These measures may include:

- **Nuclear Material Accountancy:** States parties are required to maintain a detailed record of their nuclear materials, including their production, use, and transfer. The IAEA verifies the accuracy of these records through inspections, measurements, and data analysis.

- **Physical Inspections:** The IAEA conducts inspections of declared nuclear facilities to verify their declared activities and ensure compliance with safeguards obligations. These inspections may involve the examination of nuclear material, measurement of radiation levels, and examination of operational records.
- **Containment and Surveillance:** The IAEA may install surveillance equipment, such as cameras and seals, to monitor the movement and storage of nuclear materials. These measures help ensure that nuclear materials are not diverted or used for unauthorized purposes.
- **Environmental Sampling:** The IAEA collects environmental samples to detect traces of nuclear material and activities. These samples are analyzed in laboratories to provide additional information and support the verification process.
- **Additional Protocol:** In addition to comprehensive safeguards agreements, the TPNW encourages states parties to conclude and implement an Additional Protocol with the IAEA. The Additional

Protocol grants the IAEA expanded access to information and locations within a state, enhancing the agency's ability to detect and deter any undeclared nuclear activities.

The inclusion of safeguards and verification measures in the *TPNW* serves multiple purposes. First, it ensures that states parties fulfill their obligations under the treaty by using nuclear materials and facilities exclusively for peaceful purposes. Second, it provides assurance to other states parties and the international community that nuclear weapons-related activities are effectively monitored and prevented. Finally, it contributes to the overall credibility and integrity of the treaty by demonstrating a commitment to transparency, accountability, and nonproliferation.

By incorporating safeguards and verification measures, the TPNW strengthens its implementation mechanisms and reinforces the commitment of states parties to the peaceful use of nuclear energy while preventing the diversion of nuclear materials and technologies for military purposes. These measures help build confidence among states and contribute to the overall effectiveness and credibility of the treaty.

4. Victim Assistance and Environmental Remediation: The TPNW recognizes the disproportionate impact of the use or testing of nuclear weapons on victims, including those affected by radiation, and emphasizes the importance of providing assistance, support, and rehabilitation to affected individuals and communities. It also highlights the need for environmental remediation of areas contaminated by nuclear weapon activities.

The *Treaty on the Prohibition of Nuclear Weapons (TPNW)* acknowledges the severe and long-lasting consequences of the use or testing of nuclear weapons on individuals, communities, and the environment. It places significant emphasis on victim assistance and environmental remediation as integral components of its disarmament and non-proliferation framework.

Victim Assistance: The TPNW recognizes the disproportionate impact of nuclear weapons on victims, including those affected by the immediate and long-term consequences of nuclear detonations, such as radiation exposure, physical injuries, psychological trauma, displacement, and the loss of livelihoods and communities. The treaty emphasizes the importance of providing adequate assistance, support, and rehabilitation to victims to address their specific needs and promote their well-being.

The TPNW calls upon states parties to take measures to ensure the full and equal participation of affected individuals, including survivors, in decisions related to assistance and support programs. It encourages the provision of medical care, psychological support, rehabilitation services, and socioeconomic assistance to victims. The treaty recognizes the need for specialized training and capacity-building to address the unique challenges posed by nuclear weapon-related incidents.

Environmental Remediation: The TPNW recognizes the harmful and lasting effects of nuclear weapon activities on the environment, including contamination of soil, water, and ecosystems. It emphasizes the need for environmental remediation efforts to restore affected areas to a safe and sustainable condition. Environmental remediation involves the cleanup, decontamination, and restoration of contaminated sites to minimize risks to human health and the environment.

The treaty encourages states parties to cooperate and provide assistance in environmental remediation efforts, particularly in areas where they have conducted nuclear weapon testing or other activities that have resulted in contamination. This cooperation may include technical expertise, financial support, information sharing, and capacity-building initiatives. The TPNW recognizes the importance of engaging affected communities and indigenous peoples in decision-making processes related to environmental remediation.

The inclusion of victim assistance and environmental remediation provisions in the TPNW reflects a broader recognition of the humanitarian consequences of nuclear weapons and the moral imperative to address the impacts on affected individuals and the environment. By highlighting these issues, the treaty seeks to promote a more comprehensive approach to disarmament and non-proliferation, one that acknowledges the human and environmental costs of nuclear weapons and takes concrete steps to address them.

It is important to note that the TPNW complements existing frameworks and initiatives addressing victim assistance and environmental remediation. Efforts in these areas have been ongoing through various international mechanisms, such as the United Nations' agencies, programs, and specialized institutions. The TPNW reinforces and reinforces the importance of these efforts within the specific context of nuclear weapons prohibition. Ultimately, the provisions on victim assistance and environmental remediation in the TPNW aim to promote empathy, solidarity, and the recognition of the rights and needs of those affected by nuclear weapons. They contribute to the broader goal of achieving a world free of nuclear weapons, where the devastating consequences of these weapons are acknowledged, mitigated, and prevented.

5. Positive Obligations: The treaty includes positive obligations for states parties to provide assistance to affected states, support for victim rehabilitation and environmental remediation, and promotion of disarmament education and public awareness.

The Treaty on the Prohibition of Nuclear Weapons (TPNW) goes beyond establishing prohibitions and obligations related to nuclear weapons. It also includes positive obligations for states parties to take proactive measures that contribute to disarmament, victim assistance, environmental remediation, and public awareness. These positive obligations reflect the treaty's commitment to addressing the humanitarian impact of nuclear weapons and fostering a culture of peace and disarmament.

Assistance to Affected States: The TPNW recognizes the responsibility of states parties to provide assistance and support to affected states that have suffered the consequences of the use or testing of nuclear weapons. This includes financial, technical, and humanitarian assistance to aid in recovery, rehabilitation, and reconstruction efforts. By providing assistance, states parties demonstrate solidarity and promote international cooperation to address the needs of affected states and communities.

Support for Victim Rehabilitation and Environmental Remediation: In addition to assistance provided to affected states, the TPNW emphasizes the importance of support for victim rehabilitation and environmental remediation. States parties are encouraged to provide resources and services to assist victims, including survivors, in their physical and psychological recovery. This can involve medical care, counseling, social support, and economic assistance to help individuals rebuild their lives and communities.

Furthermore, the treaty recognizes the need for environmental remediation efforts to restore areas affected by nuclear weapon activities. States parties are encouraged to support and participate in remediation programs that aim to clean up contaminated sites and mitigate the long-term environmental impacts of nuclear weapons. By doing so, they contribute to the preservation and protection of the environment and minimize the risks posed to human health and ecosystems.

Promotion of Disarmament Education and Public Awareness: The TPNW emphasizes the importance of disarmament education and public awareness in achieving its goals. States parties are encouraged to promote education and public outreach programs that raise awareness about the risks and consequences of nuclear weapons, as well as the benefits of disarmament and peaceful conflict resolution. By engaging in such activities, states parties seek to foster a culture of peace, disarmament, and non-violence among their populations.

Disarmament education and public awareness initiatives can take various forms, including educational programs in schools, awareness campaigns, public forums, and media outreach. The goal is to inform and engage individuals, communities, civil society organizations, and other stakeholders in discussions and actions related to nuclear disarmament, non-proliferation, and peacebuilding.

By incorporating positive obligations related to assistance, victim rehabilitation, environmental remediation, and public awareness, the TPNW encourages states parties to take concrete actions beyond mere compliance with prohibitions. These obligations promote a comprehensive approach to nuclear disarmament and emphasize the human dimension of disarmament efforts. They demonstrate a commitment to addressing the humanitarian consequences of nuclear weapons and building a safer and more peaceful world.

6. Entry into Force: The TPNW requires 50 states parties for its entry into force. As of September 2021, the treaty has been ratified by 54 states and has entered into force on January 22, 2021.

The entry into force of the Treaty on the Prohibition of Nuclear Weapons (TPNW) is a significant milestone in the treaty's implementation and global efforts towards nuclear disarmament. According to the treaty's provisions, it required the ratification and acceptance by 50 states parties for it to enter into force.

As of September 2021, the TPNW has been ratified by 54 states. This means that these 54 states have formally accepted the treaty's provisions and obligations, indicating their commitment to prohibiting nuclear weapons and working towards their elimination. The treaty officially entered into force on January 22, 2021, ninety days after the fiftieth ratification was achieved, as specified in its Article 15.

The entry into force of the TPNW represents a significant development in the nuclear disarmament landscape. It demonstrates the growing global support for efforts to address the humanitarian consequences of nuclear weapons and the desire for a world free of such devastating weapons. The treaty's entry into force also sends a strong signal to the international community about the urgency and importance of nuclear disarmament.

It is worth noting that the states parties that have ratified the TPNW represent a diverse range of countries from various regions. While some of these states are non-nuclear-weapon states that have long advocated for nuclear disarmament, others are countries that have been affected by the use or testing of nuclear weapons or have concerns about the humanitarian impact of these weapons. The entry into force of the TPNW reflects the collective determination of these states to take action towards nuclear disarmament and challenge the status quo.

However, it is important to acknowledge that the TPNW has not been ratified by the nine nuclear-weapon states recognized under the Treaty on the Non-Proliferation of Nuclear Weapons (NPT). These states, including the United States, Russia, the United Kingdom, France, China, India, Pakistan, Israel, and North Korea, have not joined the TPNW and have expressed reservations or opposition to its provisions.

The divide between nuclear-weapon states and non-nuclear-weapon states regarding the TPNW highlights the ongoing complexities and challenges in achieving universal adherence and consensus on nuclear disarmament. While the TPNW has gained support from a significant number of states, the participation of nuclear-weapon states remains crucial for the treaty's effectiveness and its ability to bring about tangible disarmament outcomes.

Nevertheless, the entry into force of the TPNW has already had an impact on the global discourse surrounding nuclear disarmament. It has invigorated debates, increased public awareness, and intensified discussions on the humanitarian consequences of nuclear weapons. The treaty provides a platform for dialogue and engagement between states parties, civil society organizations, and other stakeholders, fostering momentum and creating opportunities for progress in nuclear disarmament efforts.

Significance and Impact:

The TPNW has been hailed by its proponents as a landmark achievement in nuclear disarmament and non-proliferation efforts. Supporters argue that the treaty fills a legal gap by explicitly prohibiting nuclear weapons, which were not covered by existing disarmament treaties like the NPT.

The TPNW reflects the growing concerns regarding the humanitarian impact of nuclear weapons. It emphasizes the catastrophic consequences of the use of nuclear weapons, including the immense loss of human life, environmental devastation, and long-lasting health effects. The treaty seeks to stigmatize and delegitimize nuclear weapons by establishing a norm against their possession and use.

However, the TPNW has faced criticism and opposition from nuclear-weapon states and some of their allies. These states argue that the treaty does not adequately consider the complex security environment and the role of nuclear deterrence in maintaining peace and security. They contend that disarmament should be pursued through a step-by-step process within the existing framework, including the NPT.

The TPNW has also raised concerns about its relationship with existing disarmament agreements, particularly the NPT. Some states argue that the treaty's provisions may conflict with the obligations of NPT states parties, as the TPNW calls for the elimination of nuclear weapons while the NPT recognizes the right of nuclear-weapon states to possess such weapons. These concerns have led some states to choose not to join or ratify the TPNW.

While the TPNW has received significant attention and support from non-nuclear-weapon states, its impact on the nuclear disarmament landscape is yet to be fully realized. Its effectiveness in achieving nuclear disarmament and its ability to bring about significant change will depend on a range of factors, including the willingness of nuclear-weapon states to engage with the treaty and the level of international support and adherence to its provisions.

Supporters of the TPNW argue that it strengthens the norm against nuclear weapons and puts pressure on nuclear-weapon states to take concrete steps towards disarmament. They believe that the treaty creates a framework for dialogue and action, even if nuclear-weapon states are not immediate participants. They argue that the TPNW can contribute to delegitimizing nuclear weapons and increasing public awareness about the humanitarian consequences of their use.

The TPNW has also been seen as a tool to mobilize civil society and grassroots movements in advocating for nuclear disarmament. It has brought attention to the issue and sparked discussions and debates on nuclear weapons policies. The treaty has the potential to influence public opinion and shape political discourse on disarmament.

However, critics of the TPNW argue that it may have limited practical impact on nuclear-weapon states. Since the treaty was negotiated without the participation of nuclear-weapon states, they are unlikely to join or abide by its provisions. Some argue that the treaty may even undermine existing disarmament efforts, such as the NPT, by creating divisions and conflicting obligations among states.

Another concern raised by critics is the potential impact on regional security dynamics. In regions where there are ongoing conflicts or security challenges, the elimination of nuclear weapons without addressing underlying security concerns may be viewed as unrealistic or detrimental to stability. Critics argue that a step-by-step approach to disarmament, within existing frameworks, is more feasible and effective.

The relationship between the TPNW and the NPT has been a subject of debate. The TPNW is seen by some as a response to the perceived stagnation in nuclear disarmament efforts within the NPT framework. While the NPT aims for eventual disarmament, the TPNW takes a more explicit and immediate approach by calling for the prohibition and elimination of nuclear weapons. Some states have expressed concerns about potential conflicts between the obligations of NPT states parties and the provisions of the TPNW.

It is important to note that the TPNW is still in its early stages, and its impact will become clearer over time. As more states ratify the treaty, its influence may grow, and it may continue to shape the discourse on nuclear disarmament. However, achieving significant progress in disarmament will require engagement and cooperation from all relevant stakeholders, including nuclear-weapon states, non-nuclear-weapon states, and international organizations.

The Treaty on the Prohibition of Nuclear Weapons represents a significant development in global efforts to eliminate nuclear weapons. It seeks to establish a norm against nuclear weapons and emphasize the humanitarian consequences of their use. While the treaty has garnered support from many non-nuclear-weapon states, it also faces criticism and challenges from nuclear-weapon states and some of their allies. The long-term impact of the TPNW on nuclear disarmament efforts will depend on various factors, including the willingness of nuclear-weapon states to engage with the treaty and the broader international support for its objectives.

Challenges to Disarmament

Achieving disarmament, particularly in the context of nuclear weapons, is a complex and challenging endeavor that faces various obstacles and hurdles. While the goal of disarmament is widely recognized and supported by the international community, there are several challenges that impede its progress. These challenges can be categorized into political, security, technical, and perceptual factors.

1. Political Challenges:

a. Lack of Political Will: Disarmament requires a strong political will from states to pursue and prioritize the reduction and elimination of weapons. However, differing national interests, strategic concerns, and geopolitical rivalries often hinder the development of consensus and effective disarmament measures.

b. National Security Concerns: States may perceive nuclear weapons as essential for their national security, deterrence, and survival. The belief in the strategic value of these weapons and concerns about maintaining a credible deterrent can create reluctance to pursue disarmament.

c. Regional Conflicts and Tensions: Disarmament efforts can be undermined by regional conflicts and tensions. In regions where states perceive security threats, such as unresolved territorial disputes or historical rivalries, the desire to maintain a nuclear deterrent can prevail over disarmament initiatives.

2. Security Challenges:

a. Nuclear Deterrence: The concept of nuclear deterrence, based on the idea that possessing nuclear weapons can prevent conflicts and ensure stability, remains a significant challenge to disarmament. States argue that as long as other states possess nuclear weapons, they need to maintain their own deterrent capabilities.

b. Verification and Transparency: Ensuring the verification of disarmament commitments and maintaining transparency in disarmament processes are complex tasks. Developing effective verification mechanisms that guarantee compliance without compromising sensitive information is challenging.

c. Nuclear Risks and Instability: The fear of nuclear proliferation and the potential for non-state actors to acquire nuclear weapons pose significant security concerns. These risks can create a sense of insecurity, making states reluctant to disarm without strong assurances of non-proliferation.

3. Technical Challenges:

a. Disarmament Verification: Verifying the complete dismantlement of nuclear weapons and ensuring that states have fulfilled their disarmament obligations is a technical challenge. The dismantlement process requires sophisticated and reliable verification mechanisms to monitor the destruction of warheads and the elimination of nuclear materials.

b. Irreversibility: Disarmament must be irreversible to ensure that nuclear weapons cannot be reacquired or reconstructed. Achieving irreversibility requires secure storage and disposal of nuclear materials, technical expertise, and a robust system of safeguards.

c. Disarmament Technologies: Developing and implementing technologies for disarmament, such as dismantlement techniques and verification technologies, can pose technical challenges. The research, development, and deployment of these technologies require significant resources and expertise.

4. Perceptual Challenges:

a. Lack of Trust: Building trust among states is crucial for disarmament efforts. Historical mistrust, unresolved conflicts, and perceptions of inequality in disarmament obligations can hinder trust-building measures and impede progress.

b. Perception of Security Erosion: Some states may perceive disarmament as a threat to their security, fearing that relinquishing nuclear weapons may leave them vulnerable to aggression or coercion. Addressing these security concerns and providing alternative security assurances is essential.

c. Public Perception: Public opinion and domestic politics play a significant role in shaping disarmament policies.

Resistance from domestic constituencies, including defense industries, political factions, and public sentiment, can make it challenging for governments to pursue disarmament measures.

Addressing these challenges requires sustained diplomatic efforts, dialogue, confidence-building measures, and incremental steps towards disarmament. Building consensus, enhancing transparency, and addressing the security concerns of states are crucial for making progress in disarmament. International cooperation, robust verification mechanisms, and increased public awareness about the humanitarian consequences of nuclear weapons can also contribute to overcoming these challenges.

While achieving disarmament faces significant challenges, progress can be made through diplomatic efforts, dialogue, technical innovation, and confidence-building measures. Overcoming political, security, technical, and perceptual obstacles requires sustained commitment from states, international cooperation, and the engagement of civil society. By addressing these challenges collectively, the goal of a world free from the threat of nuclear weapons can be realized.

Summary

Disarmament is a critical process aimed at reducing and eliminating weapons, particularly weapons of mass destruction, to promote international peace, security, and stability. It involves the voluntary surrender, destruction, and cessation of production of weapons, as well as the establishment of confidence-building measures. Disarmament efforts require global cooperation, diplomatic negotiations, and the commitment of states to create a safer world.

Here is a brief summary and five action points based on the discussion so far:

Action Points

1. **Strengthen international disarmament frameworks:** Support and strengthen existing international disarmament frameworks, such as the Treaty on the Non-Proliferation of Nuclear Weapons (NPT) and the Chemical Weapons Convention (CWC). Encourage states to fully implement their disarmament commitments and

fulfill their obligations under these treaties.

2. **Enhance transparency and verification mechanisms:** Develop and enhance transparency measures and verification mechanisms to ensure the accurate reporting and monitoring of disarmament efforts. This includes promoting the use of international inspection regimes, verification protocols, and confidence-building measures to build trust among states.

3. **Promote multilateral negotiations and diplomacy:** Engage in multilateral negotiations and diplomatic efforts to facilitate disarmament agreements and treaties. Encourage dialogue among states to address disarmament challenges, resolve differences, and build consensus on arms control and disarmament measures.

4. **Support disarmament education and awareness:** Promote disarmament education and awareness initiatives to foster a culture of peace and disarmament. This includes raising public awareness about the dangers of weapons proliferation, the benefits of disarmament, and the need for collective action to reduce global arms

stockpiles.

5. **Allocate resources for disarmament initiatives:** Allocate sufficient resources and funding for disarmament initiatives, including programs for the safe disposal of weapons, conversion of military industries, and support for the socio-economic development of regions affected by disarmament measures. Encourage states to redirect military spending towards disarmament and peacebuilding efforts.

Chapter 4

Ethical and Moral Dilemmas - Arguments For and Against the Use of Nuclear Weapons

Arguments For the Use of Nuclear Weapons:

1. **Deterrence:** Proponents argue that nuclear weapons serve as a powerful deterrent against aggression. The possession of nuclear weapons is believed to discourage potential adversaries from initiating conflicts, as the potential consequences of a nuclear attack are catastrophic. The argument is that the mere existence of nuclear weapons prevents large-scale wars and promotes stability among nuclear-armed states.

2. **National Security:** Supporters of nuclear weapons argue that they provide a credible means of protecting a nation's security and sovereignty. They believe that possessing nuclear weapons can deter potential attacks and ensure the survival of the state. The possession of nuclear weapons is seen as an essential tool for preserving national interests and

deterring aggression from other states.

3. **Defense and Strategic Balance:** Some argue that nuclear weapons contribute to maintaining a strategic balance among nations. The possession of nuclear weapons by multiple states is perceived as preventing any one state from gaining a significant advantage over others. This balance is seen as essential for preventing major conflicts and promoting stability in international relations.

4. **Status and Prestige:** Nuclear weapons are often associated with great power status and influence on the global stage. Some argue that possessing nuclear weapons enhances a state's prestige, influence, and standing in international affairs. The possession of nuclear weapons can be seen as a symbol of technological and military prowess, providing states with a seat at the table of major powers.

Arguments Against the Use of Nuclear Weapons:

1. **Humanitarian Consequences:** Critics emphasize the devastating humanitarian impact of nuclear

weapons. The immense destructive power of nuclear weapons and their potential to cause indiscriminate and long-term harm to civilian populations are viewed as morally unacceptable. The use of nuclear weapons can lead to widespread loss of life, environmental devastation, and long-lasting health effects, making their use incompatible with humanitarian values.

2. **Global Catastrophic Risks:** Detractors argue that the use of nuclear weapons poses significant global risks, including accidental or unauthorized detonation, escalation of conflicts, and the potential for nuclear terrorism. The proliferation of nuclear weapons increases the chances of their use in a conflict or falling into the wrong hands. The catastrophic consequences of a nuclear exchange outweigh any perceived benefits.

3. **Arms Race and Proliferation:** Critics contend that the possession of nuclear weapons by some states may encourage others to pursue their own nuclear programs. This can lead to a dangerous arms race and increase the risk of nuclear proliferation, as more states seek to acquire nuclear weapons as a

means of ensuring their security. The spread of nuclear weapons undermines global non-proliferation efforts and stability.

4. **Disarmament and Peaceful Alternatives:** Opponents argue that disarmament efforts are crucial for achieving lasting peace and security. They advocate for the complete elimination of nuclear weapons through multilateral disarmament agreements. Resources and efforts could be redirected towards diplomacy, conflict resolution, and investing in peaceful alternatives to address security concerns and promote international cooperation.

5. **Environmental and Human Security:** Critics emphasize the long-term environmental consequences of nuclear weapons use, including radioactive contamination and damage to ecosystems. Additionally, the vast financial and material resources allocated to the development and maintenance of nuclear arsenals could be redirected towards addressing pressing global challenges, such as poverty, climate change, and public health.

It is important to note that the use of nuclear weapons is widely condemned under international humanitarian law, including the principles of distinction, proportionality, and the prohibition of unnecessary suffering. The majority of states support disarmament and non-proliferation efforts, recognizing the inherent risks and moral concerns associated with nuclear weapons.

Principle of Proportionality

The principle of proportionality is a fundamental concept in ethics, law, and warfare. It serves as a guiding principle to assess the appropriateness and legitimacy of actions taken during armed conflicts or in response to threats. The principle of proportionality requires that the use of force or the harm inflicted should be proportional to the objective or goal pursued.

In the context of armed conflict, the principle of proportionality is a key component of *international humanitarian law (IHL),* also known as the law of armed conflict or the laws of war. **IHL** seeks to regulate the conduct of armed conflicts and protect individuals who are not or no longer participating in hostilities, including civilians and captured combatants.

According to the principle of proportionality in IHL, parties to a conflict must make sure that the anticipated military advantage gained from an attack is not outweighed by the expected harm to civilians or civilian objects. This means that the use of force must be limited to what is necessary to achieve a legitimate military objective, and the harm caused to civilians or civilian objects must be minimized.

To apply the principle of proportionality in practice, military commanders and decision-makers must make a careful assessment of the anticipated effects of an attack. They should consider the expected military advantage, the specific military objective, and the potential harm to civilians and civilian infrastructure. If the expected harm to civilians or civilian objects is excessive in relation to the anticipated military advantage, the attack would be considered disproportionate and, therefore, illegal under IHL.

The principle of proportionality requires a balancing act between military necessity and the protection of civilian lives and infrastructure. It recognizes the inherent value of civilian life and the need to minimize harm to non-combatants. It promotes the idea that armed conflicts should be conducted with a degree of restraint and respect for the principles of humanity.

It is essential to note that the principle of proportionality does not prohibit all civilian casualties or collateral damage in armed conflicts. It recognizes that some harm to civilians or civilian objects may be unavoidable in certain military operations. However, it requires that such harm be minimized to the greatest extent possible and be proportionate to the military advantage sought.

The principle of proportionality extends beyond the laws of armed conflict and finds application in various legal, ethical, and policy contexts. In criminal law, for example, it is used to determine the appropriate punishment for a crime based on the severity of the offense. In constitutional law, it may be invoked to assess the constitutionality of a government action or policy, ensuring that the infringement on rights is proportionate to the public interest or objective pursued.

Overall, the principle of proportionality serves as an important ethical and legal framework for decision-making in situations involving the use of force. It seeks to strike a balance between military necessity and the protection of civilians, emphasizing the importance of minimizing harm and ensuring that the force used is proportionate to the objective pursued.

Health and Environmental Effects of Nuclear Testing and Accidents

Nuclear testing and accidents have had significant health and environmental effects, highlighting the dangers and risks associated with nuclear technologies. These events have resulted in immediate and long-term consequences for human health, ecosystems, and the environment. Understanding the health and environmental effects of nuclear testing and accidents is crucial for assessing the risks, implementing safety measures, and informing policies related to nuclear technologies.

1. Health Effects of Nuclear Testing:
a. Acute Effects: Nuclear tests release large amounts of radioactive materials into the atmosphere, which can lead to immediate health effects for those exposed. These effects include radiation sickness, acute radiation

syndrome, and even death. The severity of health effects depends on factors such as proximity to the test site, the size of the explosion, and weather conditions.

b. Cancer and Genetic Effects: Exposure to radiation from nuclear testing can increase the risk of developing various types of cancer, including leukemia, thyroid cancer, and solid tumors. Prolonged exposure to low doses of radiation may also lead to genetic mutations, potentially affecting future generations.

c. Long-Term Health Impacts: Nuclear testing can have long-term health effects, including increased rates of cancer and other radiation-related illnesses. Some studies suggest that individuals exposed to radiation from nuclear tests may experience health issues such as cardiovascular diseases, respiratory disorders, and reproductive problems later in life.

2. Environmental Effects of Nuclear Testing:

a. Radioactive Contamination: Nuclear testing releases radioactive isotopes into the environment, contaminating soil, water, and vegetation. These isotopes can persist for long periods and pose a threat to ecosystems and human populations. Radioactive contamination can enter the food chain, resulting in the accumulation of radioactive materials in plants, animals, and humans.

b. Ecological Disruption: Nuclear testing can disrupt ecosystems by damaging habitats, killing or displacing wildlife, and disrupting ecological processes. The release of radioactive materials can have devastating effects on plant and animal species, leading to genetic mutations, population decline, and ecosystem imbalance.

c. Long-Term Environmental Impact: The environmental impact of nuclear testing can persist for decades or even centuries. Radioactive materials can remain in the environment, affecting ecosystems and human populations long after the tests have ceased. Contaminated areas may require extensive cleanup efforts and long-term monitoring to mitigate the environmental impact.

3. Health and Environmental Effects of Nuclear Accidents:

a. Radiation Exposure: Nuclear accidents, such as the Chernobyl disaster in 1986 and the Fukushima Daiichi nuclear accident in 2011, have resulted in significant radiation exposure to workers, residents, and the environment. Acute and long-term health effects, including radiation sickness, increased cancer rates, and genetic damage, have been observed in populations affected by these accidents.

b. Contamination of Air, Water, and Soil: Nuclear accidents can release radioactive materials into the environment, contaminating air, water bodies, and soil. This contamination can have far-reaching consequences, including the spread of radioactive particles through air currents, the contamination of water sources, and the uptake of radioactive materials by plants and animals.

c. Displacement and Social Impacts: Nuclear accidents often lead to the evacuation and displacement of populations from affected areas. These displacements can have significant social, psychological, and economic impacts on individuals and communities. Displaced populations may face challenges in accessing healthcare, housing, and education, and may experience long-lasting psychological trauma.

Efforts to mitigate the health and environmental effects of nuclear testing and accidents include implementing safety measures, establishing regulations and guidelines, conducting research on radiation exposure and its effects, and providing medical and social support to affected populations. The development of international frameworks, such as the International Atomic Energy Agency's guidelines and the United Nations' programs on nuclear safety and radiation protection, aims to address these issues and promote the safe and responsible use of nuclear technologies.

Furthermore, lessons learned from past nuclear accidents and testing have led to improved safety practices and the development of advanced nuclear technologies that minimize the risks to human health and the environment. These include enhanced containment systems, improved emergency response plans, and stricter regulatory frameworks.

However, despite these efforts, the health and environmental effects of nuclear testing and accidents continue to pose challenges. Long-term monitoring and research are necessary to understand the full extent of the impacts and to develop effective strategies for mitigating the risks associated with nuclear technologies.

Additionally, public awareness and education play a

crucial role in addressing the health and environmental effects of nuclear testing and accidents. Providing accurate information about the risks, safety measures, and preventive actions can empower individuals and communities to make informed decisions and take appropriate precautions. It is important to foster open communication and transparency, ensuring that the public is well-informed and involved in discussions regarding nuclear technologies and their potential impacts.

Nuclear testing and accidents have significant health and environmental effects that cannot be ignored. The release of radioactive materials during nuclear testing and accidents can result in acute and long-term health impacts, including increased risks of cancer and genetic mutations. The contamination of air, water, and soil can disrupt ecosystems and pose risks to human populations. Efforts to mitigate these effects include implementing safety measures, conducting research, establishing regulations, and providing support to affected populations. Continued vigilance, international cooperation, and advancements in nuclear technology are necessary to minimize the risks associated with nuclear testing and accidents and to ensure the safe and responsible use of nuclear technologies.

Summary

Ethical and moral dilemmas present challenging situations where individuals must make difficult choices that involve conflicting ethical principles or moral values. These dilemmas require thoughtful reflection, consideration of the potential consequences, and a commitment to acting in accordance with one's moral compass. By acknowledging the complexities of ethical and moral dilemmas, individuals can navigate these situations with integrity and contribute to a more ethical society.

Action Points

1. **Promote ethical awareness and education**: Foster ethical awareness by providing education and training programs that equip individuals with the knowledge and skills necessary to recognize and address ethical and moral dilemmas.
2. **Encourage open dialogue and reflection:** Create spaces for open and respectful dialogue where individuals can discuss ethical and moral dilemmas, share perspectives, and engage in critical reflection

to gain deeper insights into these complex issues.

3. **Establish ethical guidelines and frameworks:** Develop and implement clear ethical guidelines and frameworks within organizations and institutions that provide guidance for decision-making in challenging situations, promoting ethical conduct and responsible behavior.

4. **Foster ethical leadership:** Encourage and promote ethical leadership by recognizing and supporting individuals who demonstrate integrity, transparency, and ethical decision-making. Effective ethical leadership sets a positive example for others and fosters a culture of ethics and accountability.

5. **Embrace ethical decision-making processes:** Encourage the use of ethical decision-making models and processes that provide a structured approach to analyzing ethical dilemmas, considering various perspectives, and making informed and responsible choices.

Chapter 5
Diplomacy - Role of Diplomacy in Resolving Conflicts and Preventing Nuclear Proliferation

Diplomacy plays a crucial role in international relations, particularly in resolving conflicts and preventing the proliferation of nuclear weapons. As a peaceful and constructive approach, diplomacy seeks to foster dialogue, negotiation, and compromise between nations, with the aim of reaching mutually acceptable solutions. This chapter will explore the multifaceted role of diplomacy in resolving conflicts and preventing nuclear proliferation, highlighting its significance in promoting peace, stability, and global security.

I. Diplomacy in Conflict Resolution:

   1. Negotiation and Mediation:
   - Diplomacy facilitates negotiations and mediations between conflicting parties, providing a platform for dialogue and the exchange of ideas.
   - Skilled diplomats act as mediators, helping

parties identify common ground, manage differences, and find mutually agreeable solutions.
- Examples: The Dayton Agreement in Bosnia and Herzegovina (1995) and the Oslo Accords between Israel and Palestine (1993) demonstrate successful diplomatic efforts in resolving conflicts.

2. **Peacekeeping** and Peacebuilding:
   - Diplomatic missions and peacekeeping operations aim to prevent, manage, and resolve conflicts through diplomatic engagement, dialogue, and negotiation.
   - Diplomats work with international organizations, regional bodies, and local stakeholders to promote peacebuilding initiatives and support post-conflict reconstruction.
   - Examples: United Nations Peacekeeping missions in Cyprus, Liberia, and East Timor have played instrumental roles in conflict resolution and peacebuilding.

3. **Track II Diplomacy:**

- Informal diplomatic channels, such as track II diplomacy, involve non-governmental actors, civil society organizations, and experts in conflict resolution.
- These initiatives complement official diplomatic efforts, fostering trust-building, dialogue, and cooperation at grassroots levels.
- Examples: The Track II diplomacy initiatives in the Israeli-Palestinian conflict, such as the Geneva Initiative and the Israel-Palestine Peace Forum, have contributed to dialogue and understanding.

II. Diplomacy in Preventing Nuclear Proliferation:
1. Arms Control and Disarmament:
- Diplomatic negotiations and treaties aim to limit the spread and reduce the stockpiles of nuclear weapons.
- Arms control agreements, such as the Treaty on the Non-Proliferation of Nuclear Weapons (NPT), seek to prevent the proliferation of nuclear weapons and promote disarmament.

- Examples: The Strategic Arms Reduction Treaties (START I, II, and III) between the United States and Russia have led to significant reductions in their respective nuclear arsenals.

2. **Non-Proliferation Regimes and Treaties:**
    - Diplomatic efforts establish non-proliferation regimes and treaties that create norms, standards, and obligations for countries regarding nuclear weapons.
    - The International Atomic Energy Agency (IAEA) plays a vital role in monitoring and verifying compliance with non-proliferation obligations.
    - Examples: The Comprehensive Nuclear-Test-Ban Treaty (CTBT) and the Iran Nuclear Deal (Joint Comprehensive Plan of Action) are significant diplomatic achievements in preventing nuclear proliferation.

3. **Diplomatic Engagement and Dialogue:**
    - Diplomacy promotes engagement and dialogue between nuclear-weapon states and

non-nuclear-weapon states, fostering trust, transparency, and cooperation.
- Diplomatic initiatives, such as the Nuclear Non-Proliferation Treaty Review Conferences, provide platforms for discussions on disarmament, non-proliferation, and peaceful uses of nuclear energy.
- Examples: The Six-Party Talks on North Korea's nuclear program and the P5+1 negotiations with Iran demonstrate the importance of diplomatic engagement in preventing nuclear proliferation.

III. Challenges and Limitations of Diplomatic Efforts:

1. **Political Obstacles and Mistrust:** Political Obstacles and mistrust between conflicting parties can hinder diplomatic efforts in resolving conflicts and preventing nuclear proliferation. Deep-rooted political differences, historical grievances, and power struggles can make it challenging to establish a common ground for negotiation. Parties may be

unwilling to compromise or trust each other, leading to stalemates in diplomatic processes.

2. **Lack of Willingness to Engage:** In some cases, conflicting parties may be unwilling to engage in diplomatic dialogue due to ideological or political reasons. This reluctance can impede the progress of conflict resolution and prevent effective measures to prevent nuclear proliferation. The absence of diplomatic engagement leaves room for misunderstandings, misinterpretations, and a heightened risk of conflict escalation.

3. **Complexity of Conflicts and Nuclear Issues:** Conflicts and nuclear proliferation issues are often complex, involving multiple stakeholders with divergent interests and perspectives. Finding a mutually acceptable solution requires addressing underlying root causes, managing competing interests, and considering the complex dynamics of power, security, and regional dynamics. Diplomatic efforts must navigate these complexities to reach sustainable resolutions.

4. **Limited Enforcement Mechanisms:** While diplomatic agreements and treaties play a crucial

role in conflict resolution and non-proliferation, their effectiveness relies on compliance and enforcement mechanisms. In some cases, parties may violate agreements or fail to adhere to their obligations, undermining the effectiveness of diplomatic efforts. Strengthening enforcement mechanisms and ensuring accountability is essential to enhance the credibility and impact of diplomatic initiatives.

5. **Geostrategic Considerations:** Geostrategic considerations and regional power dynamics can influence diplomatic efforts. The interests of major powers, their alliances, and the geopolitical landscape can impact the willingness to engage in conflict resolution and nuclear non-proliferation initiatives. Balancing competing interests and finding common ground among major players is a diplomatic challenge that requires skillful negotiation and strategic diplomacy.

Diplomacy plays a vital role in resolving conflicts and preventing nuclear proliferation by fostering dialogue, negotiation, and compromise. Through various diplomatic channels, such as negotiations, mediation, peacekeeping, and track II diplomacy, conflicts can be resolved, and nuclear proliferation risks can be mitigated. However, challenges such as political obstacles, mistrust, complexity, limited enforcement mechanisms, and geostrategic considerations pose significant hurdles to effective diplomatic efforts.

To overcome these challenges, diplomatic initiatives must focus on building trust, promoting dialogue, and addressing the underlying root causes of conflicts. Strengthening international norms, treaties, and non-proliferation regimes is essential for preventing the spread of nuclear weapons. Additionally, enhancing enforcement mechanisms and promoting transparency can ensure the credibility and effectiveness of diplomatic agreements.

Ultimately, sustained commitment, political will, and multilateral cooperation are crucial for successful diplomatic efforts in conflict resolution and nuclear non-proliferation. By prioritizing diplomatic solutions and investing in dialogue, the international community can work towards a safer and more secure world, free from the threat of conflicts and nuclear weapons.

Successes and Failures of Various Diplomatic Efforts

Diplomatic efforts have been employed throughout history as a means to resolve conflicts, promote peace, and achieve mutually beneficial outcomes. Diplomatic initiatives can take various forms, including negotiations, treaties, mediation, and dialogue between nations. While some diplomatic efforts have resulted in significant successes, others have faced challenges and fallen short of their intended goals. This essay will explore a range of diplomatic efforts, examining both their successes and failures, in order to provide a comprehensive overview of the impact and limitations of diplomacy in international relations.

1. Diplomatic Successes:

a. Cold War and Arms Control Treaties:

- Strategic Arms Limitation Talks (SALT): The SALT negotiations between the United States and the Soviet Union resulted in two significant treaties, SALT I (1972) and SALT II (1979). These agreements aimed to limit the number of strategic nuclear weapons and promote arms control. They contributed to a reduction in tensions between the superpowers and helped to ease the Cold War.

- **Intermediate-Range Nuclear Forces (INF) Treaty:** Signed in 1987 between the United States and the Soviet Union, the INF Treaty eliminated an entire class of nuclear weapons by prohibiting the production, testing, and deployment of intermediate-range missiles. This successful diplomatic effort helped to reduce the risk of nuclear conflict in Europe.

b. Peace Accords and Conflict Resolution:

- **Camp David Accords:** The Camp David Accords, signed in 1978 between Egypt and Israel, facilitated the normalization of relations between the two countries. It led to the historic peace treaty between the two nations in 1979, ending years of hostility and establishing a framework for peaceful coexistence in the region.
- **Good Friday Agreement:** The Good Friday Agreement, signed in 1998, brought an end to the decades-long conflict in Northern Ireland. The agreement established power-sharing institutions, recognized the principle of consent, and initiated a

process of disarmament. It provided a foundation for peace and stability in the region.

c. Multilateral Diplomacy:

- **Paris Agreement on Climate Change:** The Paris Agreement, adopted in 2015, brought together nearly all countries to address the global challenge of climate change. The agreement set targets for reducing greenhouse gas emissions and promoted international cooperation on adaptation and mitigation efforts. It demonstrated the effectiveness of multilateral diplomacy in addressing pressing global issues.

- **Iran Nuclear Deal (Joint Comprehensive Plan of Action):** The Iran Nuclear Deal, reached in 2015 between Iran and the P5+1 (United States, Russia, China, United Kingdom, France, and Germany), aimed to ensure the peaceful nature of Iran's nuclear program. The agreement imposed restrictions on Iran's nuclear activities in exchange for sanctions relief, demonstrating the potential of diplomatic efforts to prevent nuclear proliferation.

2. Diplomatic Failures:

a. **Failed Peace Negotiations:**
- **Israeli-Palestinian Conflict:** Despite numerous diplomatic efforts, the Israeli-Palestinian conflict has seen limited success in achieving a lasting peace agreement. Various peace negotiations, such as the Oslo Accords and the Annapolis Conference, have faced challenges, including deep-rooted mistrust, unresolved territorial issues, and competing narratives. The failure to reach a comprehensive resolution highlights the complexities and deep-seated divisions in this conflict.
- **Syrian Civil War:** Diplomatic efforts to resolve the Syrian Civil War, such as the Geneva peace talks and the Astana process, have faced significant challenges due to the involvement of multiple parties with divergent interests. Despite negotiations and ceasefires, a sustainable resolution has remained elusive, resulting in ongoing violence and humanitarian crises.

b. **Non-Compliance with International Agreements:**
- **Non-Proliferation Treaty (NPT):** While the NPT has been successful in preventing the widespread proliferation of nuclear weapons, there have been

instances of non-compliance by some states. North Korea, for example, withdrew from the NPT and pursued its nuclear weapons program, leading to increased tensions in the region. Similarly, concerns have been raised regarding Iran's compliance with the NPT and its nuclear ambitions, despite the signing of the Iran Nuclear Deal. These cases highlight the challenges of ensuring full compliance with international agreements and the limitations of diplomacy in preventing all instances of non-compliance.

c. Intractable Conflicts and Stalled Negotiations:

- **Korean Peninsula:** Diplomatic efforts to address the longstanding conflict between North Korea and South Korea, as well as the nuclear standoff with the international community, have faced significant challenges. Despite various rounds of negotiations, including the Six-Party Talks, achieving a comprehensive resolution and denuclearization of the Korean Peninsula has proven elusive. The complex geopolitical dynamics, security concerns, and divergent interests of the involved parties have hindered progress in resolving this conflict.

- **Israeli-Palestinian Conflict:** As previously mentioned, the Israeli-Palestinian conflict has seen limited success in achieving a lasting peace agreement. The failure of diplomatic efforts to address core issues such as borders, settlements, and the status of Jerusalem has resulted in ongoing tensions and periodic escalations of violence. The entrenched narratives, deep-rooted mistrust, and diverging political priorities of the parties involved have hindered the prospects for a successful resolution.

d. Lessons Learned and the Way Forward:

The successes and failures of various diplomatic efforts highlight the complexity and challenges of resolving conflicts and achieving desired outcomes through diplomacy. Several lessons can be drawn from these experiences:

1. **Diplomatic efforts require sustained commitment:** Successful diplomatic initiatives often require long-term commitment and perseverance. Achieving meaningful agreements and resolving complex conflicts may take years or

even decades of negotiations, dialogue, and trust-building measures.

Sustained commitment is a fundamental requirement for successful diplomatic efforts. Resolving conflicts and achieving meaningful agreements through diplomacy is a complex and intricate process that requires time, patience, and unwavering dedication. Diplomatic initiatives often involve negotiating with multiple parties, addressing deep-rooted grievances, and finding mutually acceptable solutions. In such cases, a long-term commitment is necessary to navigate the complexities and overcome the obstacles that arise along the way.

One reason why sustained commitment is crucial is the nature of conflicts themselves. Many conflicts have deep historical, cultural, or religious roots that have shaped the narratives, identities, and interests of the parties involved. These complex dynamics cannot be resolved overnight or through quick-fix solutions. It takes time to build trust, understand the underlying concerns and grievances, and develop innovative approaches that can address the multifaceted dimensions of a conflict.

Moreover, sustained commitment allows for the

exploration of different pathways and options. Complex conflicts often involve numerous stakeholders with varying interests and perspectives. The process of negotiation and dialogue is iterative, involving multiple rounds of discussions, proposals, and counterproposals. Through sustained commitment, diplomats can explore different avenues, test ideas, and adapt strategies as needed. This flexibility is essential for finding common ground and forging agreements that are acceptable to all parties involved.

Sustained commitment is also necessary to withstand setbacks and challenges that may arise during the diplomatic process. Negotiations can be arduous and may encounter roadblocks, disagreements, or even outright failures. However, sustained commitment allows diplomats to persevere through these obstacles, maintain open lines of communication, and re-engage in dialogue when circumstances are more conducive. It is through this resilience that breakthroughs can occur, as parties can build on previous progress and overcome the hurdles that impeded earlier negotiations.

Furthermore, long-term commitment demonstrates seriousness and credibility to the parties involved. It sends a message that the diplomatic efforts are genuine, and the parties are dedicated to finding a peaceful resolution. This commitment can help build trust, as the parties involved see that their counterparts are invested in the process and are willing to invest the necessary time and effort to achieve a mutually acceptable outcome. Sustained commitment is particularly crucial when trust is fragile or when there is a history of animosity between the parties.

In addition, sustained commitment allows for the development of personal relationships and rapport between diplomats. Diplomatic negotiations are not just about the technicalities of the issues at hand but also about building interpersonal connections. These personal relationships can help foster understanding, empathy, and a sense of common purpose. Over time, diplomats develop a deeper understanding of each other's perspectives and interests, facilitating constructive dialogue and creative problem-solving.

Finally, sustained commitment ensures that the momentum for peace is maintained. Conflicts can be volatile and subject to shifts in political climates, leadership changes, or external events. By maintaining a long-term commitment, diplomats can weather these fluctuations and ensure that progress toward resolution is not derailed. This continuity is critical for preventing the erosion of trust, maintaining the focus on the end goal, and preventing conflicts from escalating or reigniting.

ustained commitment is essential for successful diplomatic efforts. Resolving conflicts and achieving meaningful agreements through diplomacy is a challenging and time-consuming process. It requires long-term dedication, perseverance, and the willingness to navigate complexities, setbacks, and obstacles. Sustained commitment allows for the exploration of different options, the building of trust, the adaptation of strategies, and the maintenance of momentum. Ultimately, it is through this sustained commitment that diplomatic efforts can yield positive outcomes and contribute to lasting peace and stability.

2. **Multilateral approaches are crucial:** Multilateral diplomacy involving multiple parties and stakeholders can enhance the prospects of successful outcomes. Engaging a diverse range of perspectives and interests can foster cooperation, create a balance of power, and build consensus

around shared goals.

Multilateral approaches play a crucial role in diplomatic efforts by involving multiple parties and stakeholders in the negotiation and resolution of complex issues. Engaging a diverse range of perspectives and interests can enhance the prospects of successful outcomes and promote stability and cooperation. There are several reasons why multilateral diplomacy is considered essential in international relations.

Firstly, multilateralism allows for the inclusion of a broader set of perspectives and interests. In many conflicts or global challenges, multiple parties have a stake and can contribute to finding solutions. By involving various actors, such as states, international organizations, regional bodies, non-governmental organizations (NGOs), and civil society groups, multilateral diplomacy ensures that a wider range of concerns, values, and expertise are taken into account. This diversity of perspectives can help identify creative and comprehensive solutions that address the complex dimensions of the issue at hand.

Secondly, multilateral approaches create a balance of power among participants. In bilateral negotiations, power dynamics can sometimes be uneven, with one party exerting more influence or having greater leverage over the other. In contrast, multilateral diplomacy provides a platform where power is distributed among multiple actors. This balance of power reduces the chances of domination by any single party and creates a more level playing field for negotiations. It allows smaller or less powerful states to have a voice and influence in decision-making processes, which contributes to a more inclusive and equitable outcome.

Thirdly, multilateralism fosters cooperation and collective action. Many global challenges, such as climate change, terrorism, nuclear proliferation, or public health crises, require collective efforts to achieve effective solutions. Multilateral diplomacy provides a forum for states to come together, share information, coordinate policies, and pool resources. By promoting cooperation, multilateral approaches can help address common challenges more effectively than individual or isolated efforts. Through collaborative action, states can leverage their collective strength and expertise to tackle complex problems that transcend national boundaries.

Furthermore, multilateral diplomacy builds consensus and

promotes legitimacy. When multiple parties are involved in negotiations, the resulting agreements or decisions tend to carry greater legitimacy. This is because the diverse range of perspectives and interests represented in the multilateral process enhances the perception that the outcome is fair, balanced, and representative of a broader consensus. Such legitimacy is crucial for the successful implementation of agreements, as it fosters trust among participants and ensures greater compliance with the agreed-upon commitments.

Moreover, multilateral approaches provide a platform for states to engage in dialogue and build relationships. Diplomatic negotiations often involve more than just finding a resolution to a specific issue; they also provide an opportunity for states to engage in broader dialogue, exchange ideas, and build mutual understanding. Through sustained interaction and dialogue, trust can be built, relationships can be strengthened, and long-term cooperation can be fostered. These relationships can be instrumental in addressing future challenges and conflicts, as they create a foundation of trust and familiarity among states.

Lastly, multilateralism helps promote global norms and rules. Through multilateral institutions and frameworks, states can develop and uphold international norms, laws, and regulations. These norms provide a common set of standards that guide state behavior and facilitate cooperation. By participating in multilateral efforts, states contribute to the development of a rules-based international order, where conflicts are resolved peacefully, and cooperation is prioritized over unilateral actions.

Multilateral approaches are crucial in diplomatic efforts due to the many benefits they offer. Engaging a diverse range of perspectives and interests through multilateral diplomacy enhances the prospects of successful outcomes, fosters cooperation, creates a balance of power, builds consensus, promotes legitimacy, facilitates dialogue and relationship-building, and helps establish global norms and rules. By embracing multilateralism, states can work together more effectively to address complex global challenges and contribute to a more stable and prosperous world.

3. **Addressing underlying root causes is essential:** Diplomatic efforts must address the underlying root

causes of conflicts to achieve sustainable resolutions. This includes addressing issues such as identity, historical grievances, territorial disputes, and socioeconomic inequalities that contribute to tensions and hostilities. Addressing the underlying root causes of conflicts is indeed essential for achieving sustainable resolutions through diplomatic efforts. Simply addressing the symptoms or surface-level issues without tackling the deeper causes can lead to temporary or fragile agreements that may not stand the test of time. To effectively resolve conflicts, diplomatic initiatives must address various factors that contribute to tensions and hostilities, including identity, historical grievances, territorial disputes, and socioeconomic inequalities.

- **Identity:** Conflicts often arise from differences in identity, such as ethnicity, religion, or nationality, which can lead to a sense of exclusion, discrimination, or marginalization. Diplomatic efforts need to recognize and respect the identities of all parties involved, ensuring that their rights and interests are acknowledged. Promoting inclusivity, fostering dialogue that acknowledges diverse perspectives, and facilitating efforts to build trust and understanding among different groups can help address identity-based conflicts.

- **Historical Grievances:** Historical grievances rooted in past injustices, conflicts, or colonial legacies can contribute to ongoing tensions. Diplomatic initiatives should recognize and address these grievances through mechanisms such as truth and reconciliation commissions, memorialization efforts, or acknowledgment of past wrongdoings. By acknowledging and addressing historical grievances, diplomatic efforts can help build a foundation of trust and reconciliation necessary for long-term peace.
- **Territorial Disputes:** Territorial disputes over land, maritime boundaries, or resources are a common source of conflicts. Diplomatic

efforts must facilitate negotiations and mediation processes to find mutually acceptable solutions to these disputes. This may involve compromise, innovative approaches to resource sharing, or creative boundary arrangements. By addressing territorial disputes, diplomatic initiatives can remove a significant source of tension and create conditions for peaceful coexistence.

- **Socioeconomic Inequalities:** Socioeconomic inequalities, including disparities in wealth, resources, and access to opportunities, can contribute to social unrest and conflict. Diplomatic efforts should address these inequalities by promoting inclusive economic growth, poverty reduction, and equitable distribution of resources. By addressing socioeconomic disparities, diplomatic initiatives can help create a more stable and harmonious environment, reducing the likelihood of conflicts driven by economic grievances.

Addressing the underlying root causes requires a comprehensive and holistic approach that goes beyond immediate concerns. It involves long-term engagement, investment in social and economic development, and a commitment to promoting justice, equality, and human rights. Diplomatic efforts should be accompanied by initiatives that promote education, healthcare, infrastructure development, and sustainable economic opportunities, particularly in conflict-affected areas. By improving living conditions and addressing socioeconomic inequalities, diplomatic initiatives can contribute to the establishment of a foundation for peace and stability.

Furthermore, it is crucial to engage all relevant stakeholders in the diplomatic process. This includes representatives from affected communities, civil society organizations, and marginalized groups. By ensuring the participation and representation of diverse voices, diplomatic efforts can take into account the perspectives and concerns of all parties involved, thereby increasing the likelihood of reaching sustainable resolutions.

Addressing the underlying root causes of conflicts is a challenging task that requires sustained commitment, resources, and cooperation among the parties involved. It may not yield immediate results, as it often involves long-term processes of reconciliation, institutional reforms, and social transformation. However, by addressing these root causes, diplomatic efforts can contribute to the development of more resilient and lasting peace, promoting stability, prosperity, and justice for all parties involved.

Diplomatic efforts must prioritize addressing the underlying root causes of conflicts to achieve sustainable resolutions. By addressing identity, historical grievances, territorial disputes, and socioeconomic inequalities, diplomatic initiatives can foster trust, reconciliation, and social transformation necessary for long-term peace. This requires comprehensive approaches that go beyond surface-level issues and engage all relevant stakeholders in the process. Through sustained commitment and cooperation, diplomatic efforts can contribute to the establishment of a more peaceful and just world.

4. **Continuous dialogue and diplomacy are necessary:** Even in the face of setbacks and failures, diplomatic channels must remain open. Continued

dialogue and engagement can help prevent further escalations, maintain lines of communication, and provide opportunities for future breakthroughs. Continuous dialogue and diplomacy play a crucial role in resolving conflicts and promoting peaceful resolutions. Even when faced with setbacks and failures, it is essential to keep diplomatic channels open and maintain ongoing engagement between conflicting parties. This commitment to continuous dialogue offers several benefits and opportunities for conflict resolution.

- **Preventing Escalation:** By keeping diplomatic channels open, parties involved in a conflict have a platform for communication and negotiation. This can help prevent further escalations, as dialogue allows for the expression of grievances, concerns, and interests in a peaceful and constructive manner. Without ongoing diplomatic efforts, conflicts may escalate into violence, leading to greater human suffering and destruction.
- **Building Trust and Understanding:** Continuous dialogue provides an opportunity to build trust and understanding between

conflicting parties. Through sustained engagement, parties can develop a better understanding of each other's perspectives, concerns, and aspirations. This understanding is crucial for finding common ground, identifying shared interests, and exploring potential solutions that can address the underlying issues of the conflict.

- **Seizing Opportunities for Breakthroughs:** While diplomatic efforts may encounter setbacks and failures, maintaining continuous dialogue creates opportunities for future breakthroughs. Over time, new circumstances, changing leadership, or shifts in geopolitical dynamics may present new possibilities for resolution. By remaining engaged and committed to diplomatic efforts, parties can seize these opportunities and make progress toward peaceful outcomes.
- **Mediation and Facilitation:** Continuous dialogue allows for the involvement of mediators or facilitators who can assist in the

negotiation process. Mediators bring impartiality, expertise, and creative problem-solving skills to the table, helping conflicting parties find common ground and overcome obstacles. Their presence can help bridge gaps, manage conflicts of interest, and guide parties toward mutually acceptable solutions.

- **Building Networks and Alliances:** Continuous dialogue provides an opportunity to build networks and alliances among nations and international organizations. Through sustained engagement, diplomatic efforts can foster relationships, establish trust, and promote cooperation. These networks and alliances can serve as support systems, offering resources, expertise, and mediation services when needed.

- **Confidence-Building Measures:** Continuous dialogue enables the implementation of confidence-building measures (CBMs). CBMs are steps taken by conflicting parties to build trust, reduce tensions, and demonstrate their commitment to peaceful resolutions. Examples of CBMs include ceasefires, prisoner exchanges, joint development projects, and cultural exchanges. These measures can create a positive momentum and lay the groundwork for broader peace-building efforts.

- **Learning from Failures:** Continuous dialogue provides an opportunity for reflection and learning from past failures. By analyzing previous diplomatic efforts, parties can identify shortcomings, understand the reasons for failure, and adjust their strategies accordingly. This iterative learning process can help refine diplomatic approaches and increase the chances of success in future negotiations.

- **International Norms and Pressure:** Continuous dialogue contributes to the formation and reinforcement of international norms and pressure for peaceful resolutions. When conflicts receive ongoing diplomatic attention, the international community is more likely to monitor the situation closely, exert diplomatic pressure on conflicting parties, and support efforts for a peaceful resolution. The sustained involvement of the international community can act as an incentive for parties to engage in diplomatic processes seriously.

Continuous dialogue and diplomacy are crucial for conflict resolution. Even in the face of setbacks and failures, it is essential to keep diplomatic channels open. Ongoing engagement provides opportunities for preventing escalation, building trust, seizing breakthroughs, utilizing mediation, building networks, implementing confidence-building measures, learning from failures, and mobilizing international norms and pressure. By maintaining dialogue, conflicting parties increase their chances of finding peaceful resolutions and contribute to the broader goal of creating a more peaceful and just world.

5. **Balancing national interests and international cooperation:** Diplomatic efforts often require finding a delicate balance between pursuing national interests and promoting international

cooperation. Negotiating compromises, building trust, and prioritizing common goals are key to achieving successful outcomes.

Balancing national interests and international cooperation is a fundamental aspect of diplomatic efforts. In any negotiation or diplomatic process, states are driven by their own national interests, which can sometimes be at odds with the interests of other nations. However, successful diplomatic initiatives require finding a delicate balance between pursuing national interests and promoting international cooperation. Here's how this balance can be achieved:

- **Negotiating Compromises:** Diplomatic efforts often involve negotiating compromises that accommodate the interests of multiple parties. This requires a willingness to give and take, as well as a recognition that achieving a mutually beneficial outcome may require making concessions. By finding common ground and striking compromises, conflicting parties can advance their respective national interests while also fostering cooperation and resolving conflicts.

- **Building Trust:** Trust is a vital component of successful diplomatic efforts. Parties involved must believe that their counterparts are genuinely committed to finding mutually acceptable solutions. Building trust requires transparency, open communication, and demonstrating a willingness to fulfill commitments. When trust is established, conflicting parties are more likely to engage in cooperative efforts, allowing for the pursuit of national interests within a framework of mutual respect and understanding.

- **Prioritizing Common Goals:** Diplomatic efforts are more likely to succeed when conflicting parties recognize and prioritize common goals that transcend narrow national interests. Identifying shared objectives, such as regional stability, economic development, or environmental sustainability, can create a foundation for cooperation. By aligning national interests with broader global challenges, states can see the value in pursuing collaborative solutions that benefit not only themselves but also the international community as a whole.

- **Developing Long-Term Strategies**: Balancing national interests and international cooperation requires taking a long-term perspective. Short-term gains that solely serve immediate national interests can undermine long-term prospects for cooperation and stability. Diplomatic efforts should focus on developing strategies that take into account the evolving global landscape, anticipate potential challenges, and promote sustainable outcomes. By adopting a forward-looking approach, states can balance their national interests with the need for international cooperation.
- **Engaging in Multilateralism:** Multilateralism plays a crucial role in balancing national interests and international

cooperation. Engaging in multilateral forums, such as the United Nations, regional organizations, or international treaties, allows states to negotiate and coordinate actions based on shared principles and objectives. Multilateral approaches provide a platform for addressing global challenges, pooling resources, and fostering cooperation, thereby ensuring that national interests are pursued within a broader framework of collective action.

- **Recognizing Interdependence:** Diplomatic efforts must acknowledge the interdependence of states in an increasingly interconnected world. Global challenges, such as climate change, terrorism, or pandemics, require collective responses that go beyond national boundaries. Recognizing this interdependence helps states understand that pursuing narrow national interests without considering the broader implications can have detrimental consequences. By acknowledging the interconnections between states, diplomatic efforts can prioritize international cooperation and collaboration.

- **Building Coalitions and Alliances:** In the pursuit of national interests, states can leverage alliances and coalitions to enhance their bargaining power and promote shared objectives. Diplomatic efforts can focus on building alliances based on mutual interests, common values, or regional cooperation. By forging partnerships, states can strengthen their position while also contributing to broader international cooperation and stability.

Achieving a balance between national interests and international cooperation is essential for successful diplomatic efforts. Negotiating compromises, building trust, prioritizing common goals, developing long-term strategies, engaging in multilateralism, recognizing interdependence, and building coalitions and alliances are all strategies that help navigate this delicate balance. By finding ways to reconcile national interests with the broader global agenda, states can contribute to a more cooperative and interconnected world, where conflicts are resolved, and common challenges are addressed through diplomatic means.

Moving forward, diplomatic efforts should continue to play a central role in resolving conflicts and preventing nuclear proliferation. Enhancing diplomatic capacities, investing in mediation and conflict resolution mechanisms, and strengthening international institutions can contribute to more effective diplomatic initiatives. Additionally, addressing the root causes of conflicts, engaging civil society, and promoting dialogue at various levels of society can help build sustainable peace and prevent the escalation of conflicts.

The successes and failures of various diplomatic efforts demonstrate both the potential and limitations of diplomacy in resolving conflicts and achieving desired outcomes. While notable achievements have been made in arms control, peace accords, and multilateral agreements, challenges remain in addressing intractable conflicts and ensuring full compliance with international agreements. By learning from past experiences, maintaining open channels of communication, and committing to sustained diplomatic efforts, the international community can continue to strive for peaceful resolutions and prevent the proliferation of nuclear weapons

Importance of Communication and Cooperation Among Nations

Communication and cooperation among nations play a crucial role in shaping the global community. As the world becomes increasingly interconnected, it becomes more important than ever to maintain open lines of communication and foster cooperation between countries. This essay will explore the importance of communication and cooperation among nations, highlighting their significance in promoting peace, prosperity, and global development.

I. Importance of Communication among Nations:

1. **Diplomacy:**

Diplomatic communication is a crucial tool for promoting understanding, resolving conflicts, and building partnerships between nations. Diplomatic communication involves the exchange of information, ideas, and opinions between diplomats and government officials from different countries. Skilled diplomats can use their communication skills to manage conflicts, establish common ground, and build trust between nations.

2. Economic Cooperation:

International trade and commerce rely on open communication between countries. Business deals, trade agreements, and investment opportunities all require effective communication and negotiation. By communicating effectively, countries can establish mutually beneficial economic relationships that can help to stimulate growth and create new opportunities for people around the world.

3. Cultural Exchange:

Cultural exchange programs promote communication and understanding between nations by facilitating exchanges of people, ideas, and traditions. These programs provide opportunities for people from different countries to learn about each other's cultures and traditions, fostering greater understanding and appreciation of cultural diversity. By building bridges between cultures, nations can promote peace and understanding.

II. Importance of Cooperation among Nations:

1. **Peace and Security:**

Cooperation among nations is essential for promoting peace and security around the world. By working together, countries can pool their resources, share information, and develop strategies for addressing common security challenges, such as terrorism, cyber threats, and nuclear proliferation. Cooperation also plays a key role in peacekeeping efforts, as countries work together to prevent conflicts from escalating and to resolve existing conflicts peacefully.

2. **Global Development:**

Cooperation among nations is also essential for promoting global development and reducing poverty around the world. Through international aid and development programs, countries can provide resources and support to developing countries, helping them to build infrastructure, improve health and education systems, and promote economic growth. By working together, countries can leverage their collective resources to make a positive impact on the lives of people around the world.

3. **Environmental Protection:**

Environmental protection is a global challenge that

requires cooperation and collaboration among nations. By working together, countries can establish common goals, develop shared strategies, and coordinate efforts to address climate change, protect biodiversity, and reduce pollution. Cooperation is also essential for managing shared natural resources, such as water, forests, and oceans, and for promoting sustainable development practices.

III. Challenges to Communication and Cooperation among Nations:

Despite the importance of communication and cooperation among nations, there are significant challenges that can impede progress in these areas. Some of the key challenges include:

1. Political Tensions:

Political tensions between countries can make it difficult to establish effective communication and cooperation. Ideological differences, territorial disputes, and historical grievances can all contribute to mistrust and hostility between nations.

Political tensions between countries can pose significant challenges to effective communication and cooperation. These tensions arise due to a variety of factors, including ideological differences, territorial disputes, and historical grievances. When political tensions exist, nations often find it difficult to engage in open and constructive dialogue, hindering the establishment of effective communication channels and impeding cooperation efforts.

Ideological differences play a significant role in political tensions between nations. Varying political systems, ideologies, and values can create fundamental differences in how countries perceive and approach global issues. These differences can result in divergent interests and objectives, making it challenging to find common ground and reach mutually acceptable solutions. Ideological conflicts can lead to mistrust and suspicion, undermining the willingness to engage in meaningful communication and cooperation.

Territorial disputes are another common source of political tensions. Conflicting claims over land, maritime boundaries, or resources can fuel deep-rooted rivalries and contribute to heightened tensions between countries. Disputes over territories often involve issues of national sovereignty, historical narratives, and national pride, making them emotionally charged and difficult to resolve. In such situations, effective communication and cooperation become even more challenging as parties become entrenched in their positions and are unwilling to compromise.

Historical grievances also contribute to political tensions between nations. Past conflicts, colonial legacies, and unresolved historical injustices can create deep-seated animosities that persist over generations. These grievances can shape national identities and influence perceptions of other countries. When historical grievances remain unaddressed, they can fuel resentment and distrust, hindering effective communication and cooperation.

The impact of political tensions on communication and cooperation among nations is significant. These tensions often result in strained diplomatic relations, limited dialogue, and the breakdown of diplomatic channels. When communication is hindered, misunderstandings and misinterpretations can arise, leading to further escalation of tensions. Moreover, political tensions can undermine trust and create a hostile atmosphere, making it challenging for countries to find common ground and work together towards shared goals.

Overcoming political tensions requires proactive efforts from all parties involved. Diplomatic initiatives, such as dialogue and negotiation, can help foster understanding and bridge ideological differences. Confidence-building measures, such as track II diplomacy or informal dialogues, can provide platforms for open and frank discussions outside formal diplomatic channels. Mediation and facilitation by neutral third parties can also play a crucial role in helping countries overcome political tensions and find mutually acceptable solutions.

Building trust is essential in addressing political tensions. Transparency, sincerity, and commitment to dialogue are vital in fostering trust among nations. Confidence-building measures, such as arms control agreements, can help alleviate security concerns and create an atmosphere conducive to communication and cooperation. Additionally, efforts to promote people-to-people exchanges, cultural diplomacy, and educational programs can help bridge divides, promote understanding, and reduce prejudices.

International organizations and regional forums also have a role to play in mitigating political tensions. These platforms provide neutral spaces for dialogue, negotiation, and conflict resolution. They can facilitate discussions on sensitive issues and provide a framework for addressing political tensions in a structured and diplomatic manner. By fostering multilateral cooperation, these organizations can promote dialogue and cooperation, even in the face of political tensions.

In conclusion, political tensions pose significant challenges to effective communication and cooperation among nations. Ideological differences, territorial disputes, and historical grievances can create mistrust and hostility, hindering the establishment of open and constructive dialogue. Overcoming political tensions requires proactive efforts, including diplomacy, confidence-building measures, and trust-building initiatives. By addressing political tensions, nations can create an environment conducive to effective communication and cooperation, paving the way for conflict resolution and the promotion of peace and stability.

2. Economic Interests:

Economic interests can also create obstacles to cooperation among nations. Countries may be reluctant to share resources or collaborate on economic issues if they perceive that doing so would threaten their own economic interests.

Economic interests can indeed create obstacles to cooperation among nations, as countries often prioritize their own economic well-being and may be reluctant to engage in collaboration if they perceive it as a threat to their interests. The pursuit of economic interests can lead to competition, protectionism, and limited cooperation, hindering the establishment of effective communication channels and impeding collective efforts for mutual benefit.

One of the main reasons economic interests can pose challenges to cooperation is the concept of national self-interest. Countries strive to maximize their economic gains, protect their domestic industries, and secure resources necessary for their development. In this pursuit, nations may adopt protectionist measures, such as tariffs, quotas, or subsidies, to shield their industries from foreign competition and safeguard their domestic markets. While such measures aim to protect national interests, they can hinder international cooperation and impede the flow of goods, services, and investments.

Disparities in economic power and wealth can also contribute to challenges in cooperation. Developed countries, with more advanced economies and greater access to resources, may be reluctant to share their advantages with developing nations. This can create a perception of unequal gains in cooperative efforts, leading to skepticism and resistance to collaboration. Developing countries, on the other hand, may feel marginalized or disadvantaged, further hindering their willingness to engage in cooperation.

Resource competition is another factor that can impede economic cooperation. Natural resources, such as oil, minerals, or water, are essential for economic development and national security. Countries may be hesitant to share or collaborate on the management and distribution of these resources if they fear that it could compromise their own access or control. Disputes over resource-rich territories or conflicting claims can escalate tensions and undermine cooperation efforts.

Additionally, economic interests can be influenced by geopolitical considerations. Countries may prioritize alliances or strategic partnerships that align with their geopolitical interests, even if it means limiting cooperation with other nations. Political considerations, such as concerns over regional influence or security, can overshadow economic cooperation and create divisions among countries.

Overcoming economic interests as obstacles to cooperation requires finding common ground and creating incentives for collaboration. One approach is to emphasize the long-term benefits and mutual gains of cooperation. By highlighting the potential economic benefits, such as increased trade, investment opportunities, and market access, countries can be incentivized to overcome their reluctance and engage in cooperative efforts.

International agreements and organizations also play a crucial role in addressing economic interests and promoting cooperation. Trade agreements, such as free trade agreements or regional economic integration initiatives, can provide a framework for countries to collaborate and remove barriers to trade and investment. International organizations, such as the World Trade Organization (WTO) and the World Bank, can facilitate negotiations, provide technical assistance, and promote fair and inclusive economic cooperation.

Furthermore, dialogue and negotiation are essential in addressing economic interests and finding common ground. Diplomatic channels, bilateral or multilateral dialogues, and summit meetings can provide platforms for countries to discuss their economic concerns, negotiate mutually beneficial solutions, and build trust. Through constructive engagement, countries can identify shared interests, address disparities, and develop frameworks for economic cooperation that consider the concerns and interests of all parties involved.

Economic interests can present challenges to cooperation among nations. National self-interest, competition, disparities in economic power, resource competition, and geopolitical considerations can all hinder collaboration. Overcoming these obstacles requires emphasizing mutual benefits, creating incentives for cooperation, and fostering dialogue and negotiation. By finding common ground and addressing concerns, countries can promote economic cooperation that benefits all parties involved and contributes to global prosperity and development.

3. Cultural Differences:

Cultural differences can also create barriers to communication and cooperation among nations.

Differences in language, values, and customs can make it difficult for people from different countries to understand each other and work effectively together. Cultural differences can indeed create barriers to communication and cooperation among nations. These differences encompass various aspects, including language, values, customs, traditions, and social norms. When people from different cultures come together, they bring with them their unique perspectives and ways of interacting with the world. While cultural diversity enriches the global community, it can also pose challenges in terms of effective communication and collaboration.

One of the primary challenges stemming from cultural differences is language barriers. Language serves as a medium for communication and understanding, and when there is a lack of a common language, it can hinder effective communication. Misinterpretations, misunderstandings, and communication breakdowns can occur when individuals do not have a shared language. This can impede the exchange of ideas, hinder negotiations, and make it difficult to establish trust and rapport between individuals from different cultural backgrounds.

Values and beliefs also differ across cultures, which can lead to clashes or disagreements when attempting to find common ground. Different societies may prioritize different principles, such as individualism versus collectivism, or place varying emphasis on concepts like time, hierarchy, or social harmony. These divergent values can result in contrasting approaches to problem-solving, decision-making, and cooperation. Without a mutual understanding and appreciation of these differences, it can be challenging to reach consensus or develop cooperative strategies.

Customs and traditions play a significant role in shaping behavior and social interactions within a culture. Etiquette, gestures, and social norms can vary significantly between countries, and what is considered acceptable in one culture may be seen as inappropriate or offensive in another. These differences can create misunderstandings, strain relationships, and hinder effective collaboration. Without a deep understanding of cultural customs and the ability to navigate cultural sensitivities, individuals may inadvertently cause offense or overlook important cultural nuances.

Moreover, cultural differences can influence communication styles and preferences. Direct versus indirect communication, high-context versus low-context communication, and the use of nonverbal cues can all vary across cultures. For instance, some cultures may value direct and explicit communication, while others may prioritize indirect communication and rely heavily on nonverbal cues. These divergent communication styles can lead to misunderstandings and misinterpretations, making effective communication and cooperation more challenging.

To overcome cultural barriers to communication and cooperation, it is crucial to foster cultural sensitivity, understanding, and intercultural competence.
This involves developing an awareness and appreciation of different cultural perspectives, norms, and communication styles. Some approaches to bridge cultural differences and enhance communication include:

1. **Cultural Training and Education:** Providing cultural training and education to individuals and organizations can help promote understanding and

awareness of different cultures. This includes learning about cultural customs, norms, and communication styles, as well as developing strategies for effective cross-cultural communication.

2. **Intermediaries and Cultural Brokers:** Engaging intermediaries or cultural brokers who have an understanding of both cultures can facilitate communication and help bridge the gap between different cultural perspectives. These individuals can serve as interpreters, mediators, or facilitators, helping to ensure effective communication and mutual understanding.

3. **Active Listening and Empathy:** Actively listening to and empathizing with individuals from different cultural backgrounds can foster understanding and build rapport. This involves being open-minded, suspending judgments, and making an effort to understand the cultural context and perspective of others.

4. **Flexibility and Adaptability:** Being flexible and adaptable in communication and behavior can help navigate cultural differences. Recognizing that

different cultures have diverse approaches and adjusting one's communication style and behaviors accordingly can facilitate smoother interactions and foster cooperation.

5. **Building Relationships and Trust:** Investing time and effort in building relationships and trust with individuals from different cultures can enhance communication and cooperation. This involves demonstrating respect, valuing diversity, and finding common ground to establish a foundation for collaboration.

By recognizing and addressing cultural differences, countries can bridge divides, promote understanding, Communication and cooperation among nations are essential for the promotion of peace, prosperity, and global development. Effective communication through diplomacy, economic cooperation, and cultural exchange allows nations to understand each other better, resolve conflicts, and build trust. Cooperation among nations is crucial for addressing global challenges such as peace and security, economic development, and environmental protection.

However, there are challenges that need to be overcome for effective communication and cooperation to take place. Political tensions, economic interests, and cultural differences can hinder the establishment of effective communication channels and hinder cooperation efforts. It is important for nations to recognize these challenges and work towards finding common ground and mutual understanding.

To foster communication and cooperation among nations, it is necessary to promote dialogue, mutual respect, and understanding. Diplomatic efforts should focus on building bridges and finding shared interests rather than emphasizing differences. Economic cooperation should be based on fairness, transparency, and mutual benefits, ensuring that all parties involved can prosper. Cultural exchange programs should be encouraged to promote cross-cultural understanding and appreciation.

Furthermore, international organizations and forums play a significant role in facilitating communication and cooperation among nations. Platforms such as the United Nations, regional organizations, and bilateral partnerships provide avenues for dialogue, negotiation, and collaboration. These platforms help create a framework for addressing global issues and building consensus among nations.

In a world that is increasingly interconnected, the importance of communication and cooperation among nations cannot be overstated. By promoting dialogue, understanding, and collaboration, nations can work together to address common challenges, resolve conflicts, and promote peace, prosperity, and sustainable development. It is through effective communication and cooperation that the global community can navigate complex issues and build a better future for all.

Summary

Diplomacy is a vital tool for managing international relations and resolving conflicts through peaceful means. It involves dialogue, negotiation, and compromise, with the goal of achieving mutually beneficial outcomes and maintaining stability in the international system. Effective diplomacy fosters trust, builds relationships, and promotes cooperation among nations, contributing to a more peaceful and prosperous world.

Action Points

1. **Prioritize diplomatic engagement:** Governments should prioritize diplomatic efforts and allocate resources to build diplomatic capacities, establish diplomatic channels, and engage in meaningful dialogue with other nations.
2. **Enhance diplomatic training and education:** Invest in training and education programs that enhance diplomats' skills in negotiation, conflict resolution, cultural understanding, and communication to ensure their effectiveness in representing their countries' interests.
3. **Strengthen multilateral diplomacy:** Actively engage in multilateral organizations, such as the United Nations, regional forums, and international treaties, to address global challenges collaboratively and promote shared solutions.
4. **Foster dialogue and mediation:** Actively promote dialogue and mediation as preferred methods for resolving conflicts, encouraging all parties to engage in constructive discussions and find common ground.

5. **Embrace diplomacy in crisis management:** Prioritize diplomatic approaches in crisis management situations, seeking diplomatic solutions over military actions whenever possible. Utilize diplomatic channels to de-escalate tensions, mediate disputes, and prevent conflicts from escalating into violence.

Chapter 6

Complexity of Nuclear Politics - Multifaceted Nature of Nuclear Politics

The topic of nuclear politics encompasses a complex and multifaceted set of issues related to the development, deployment, and use of nuclear weapons, as well as the global governance and diplomacy surrounding nuclear technology. This essay will explore the multifaceted nature of nuclear politics, examining its various dimensions, challenges, and implications in the international arena.

I. Historical Context and Evolution of Nuclear Politics:

The advent of nuclear weapons during World War II marked a turning point in international relations and set the stage for the multifaceted nature of nuclear politics. The use of atomic bombs in Hiroshima and Nagasaki demonstrated the immense destructive power of nuclear weapons, leading to a global recognition of the need for nuclear governance and nonproliferation efforts.

The Cold War between the United States and the Soviet

Union intensified nuclear politics, as the two superpowers engaged in a nuclear arms race. The development and deployment of nuclear arsenals by these states shaped global security dynamics and brought nuclear weapons to the forefront of international politics. The fear of *mutually assured destruction (MAD)* and the policy of deterrence emerged as key concepts in nuclear politics during this era.

II. Nuclear Weapons and Security:

One dimension of nuclear politics revolves around the role of nuclear weapons in ensuring national security. States possessing nuclear weapons argue that these capabilities act as a deterrent against potential adversaries and help maintain peace through the principle of mutually assured destruction. Nuclear weapons are seen as tools to prevent aggression and protect national interests.

However, this perspective is not without controversy. Critics argue that the possession and reliance on nuclear weapons create a precarious security environment, where the risk of accidental or unauthorized use, miscalculations, or escalation cannot be eliminated. The possession of nuclear weapons by multiple states introduces complexities and uncertainties in international security calculations.

III. Nuclear Non-Proliferation and Arms Control:

Another crucial dimension of nuclear politics is the non-proliferation of nuclear weapons and arms control efforts. The international community has pursued various initiatives to prevent the spread of nuclear weapons and reduce existing arsenals.

The Treaty on the *Non-Proliferation of Nuclear Weapons (NPT)*, which entered into force in 1970, serves as the cornerstone of nonproliferation efforts. It aims to prevent the spread of nuclear weapons, promote disarmament, and facilitate the peaceful use of nuclear energy. The NPT establishes a framework for nuclear-weapon states to disarm while allowing non-nuclear-weapon states to access nuclear technology for peaceful purposes under safeguards.

Arms control agreements and treaties have also been crucial in managing nuclear arsenals. Treaties like the *Strategic Arms Reduction Treaty (START)* between the United States and Russia have aimed to limit the number of deployed strategic nuclear weapons and enhance transparency and verification measures. These agreements contribute to stability and confidence-building among nuclear-weapon states.

IV. Nuclear Energy and Non-Proliferation Concerns:

The peaceful use of nuclear energy for electricity generation and other civilian purposes is another dimension of nuclear politics. The desire to harness nuclear energy for economic development has driven many countries to pursue nuclear power programs. However, the dual-use nature of nuclear technology raises concerns about the proliferation of nuclear weapons.

The international community has developed safeguards and mechanisms, primarily overseen by the *International Atomic Energy Agency (IAEA)*, to ensure the peaceful use of nuclear energy and prevent its diversion for military purposes. The proliferation risks associated with nuclear energy programs require comprehensive and effective nonproliferation measures, including rigorous inspections, export controls, and cooperation between states.

V. Nuclear Disarmament and Global Zero:

Nuclear disarmament remains a central objective of nuclear

politics. The complete elimination of nuclear weapons has been advocated by various governments, civil society organizations, and international initiatives. The Global Zero movement, for instance, seeks the total elimination of nuclear weapons through a step-by-step process and multilateral negotiations.

Achieving nuclear disarmament, however, faces significant challenges. Nuclear-weapon states may not be willing to give up their arsenals, citing security concerns and the need to deter potential adversaries. The disarmament process requires a high level of trust, transparency, and verification measures, which can be challenging to achieve in a complex and competitive international environment.

VI. Nuclear Terrorism and Security:

The threat of nuclear terrorism poses a significant challenge to global security and has added a new dimension to nuclear politics. Non-state actors, such as terrorist groups, may seek to acquire nuclear weapons or materials and use them to carry out attacks.

Efforts to prevent nuclear terrorism require cooperation and coordination among states, as well as effective border controls, intelligence sharing, and nuclear security measures. The international community has developed various mechanisms, such as the Nuclear Security Summit and the Global Initiative to Combat Nuclear Terrorism, to address this threat.

VII. Nuclear Diplomacy and International Relations:

Nuclear politics also shapes international relations and diplomacy. The possession and development of nuclear weapons are often used as leverage in diplomatic negotiations, as seen in the case of North Korea and Iran. The negotiations around the Joint Comprehensive Plan of Action (JCPOA) with Iran, for instance, involved complex and intense diplomatic efforts among multiple stakeholders.

Nuclear politics also influences alliances and security arrangements among states. The extended deterrence offered by nuclear-weapon states to their allies serves as a critical factor in maintaining regional and global stability. However, such arrangements can also create tensions and trigger arms races among states.

VIII. Ethical and Moral Dimensions of Nuclear Politics:

The multifaceted nature of nuclear politics also raises ethical and moral questions. The use of nuclear weapons in the past and the potential consequences of their use in the future raise profound moral dilemmas. The ethical implications of possessing nuclear weapons and the impact of nuclear policies on human lives and the environment are crucial considerations in nuclear politics.

The multifaceted nature of nuclear politics encompasses a range of issues, from the security dynamics of nuclear weapons to the governance and diplomacy surrounding nuclear technology. Nuclear politics is shaped by historical events, global security concerns, and the pursuit of economic and political interests by states. The complexities and challenges of nuclear politics require cooperation, dialogue, and trust-building among states, as well as effective nonproliferation and disarmament measures. Ultimately, the ethical and moral dimensions of nuclear politics demand a commitment to ensuring the safety and security of all individuals and the planet as a whole.

Difficulty of finding solutions

The difficulty of finding solutions is a common challenge encountered in various domains, ranging from personal dilemmas to complex global issues. It arises from the inherent complexity, competing interests, and diverse perspectives involved in problem-solving processes. This essay will explore the factors that contribute to the difficulty of finding solutions, including the complexity of problems, conflicting interests, cognitive biases, and the role of uncertainty.

I. Complexity of Problems:

Many problems faced by individuals, organizations, and societies are inherently complex, involving multiple interrelated factors and variables. Complex problems do not have simple or straightforward solutions and often require comprehensive analysis and understanding. The intricate nature of these problems can make it challenging to identify the underlying causes and develop effective strategies for resolution.

Complexity can arise from various sources, such as the involvement of multiple stakeholders with different perspectives and interests, the presence of interconnected systems and feedback loops, or the existence of uncertain and dynamic environments. Dealing with complex problems requires holistic thinking, systems analysis, and interdisciplinary approaches to capture the full range of factors at play.

II. Conflicting Interests:

Finding solutions becomes more difficult when there are conflicting interests among stakeholders involved in the problem. Different individuals, groups, or organizations may have divergent goals, priorities, and values, leading to competing agendas and perspectives. These conflicting interests can hinder collaboration and compromise, making it challenging to reach consensus or develop mutually acceptable solutions.

Conflicting interests often arise due to differences in power dynamics, resource distribution, cultural or ideological beliefs, or historical grievances. Resolving conflicts and finding common ground requires effective communication, negotiation, and mediation processes to bridge the gaps and foster a spirit of cooperation.

III. Cognitive Biases:

Human beings are subject to various cognitive biases that can impede the search for solutions. Cognitive biases are systematic patterns of deviation from rationality or objective judgment, resulting from mental shortcuts, heuristics, or ingrained beliefs. These biases can influence decision-making, perception of information, and evaluation of options, leading to suboptimal or biased solutions.

Examples of cognitive biases include confirmation bias, where individuals tend to seek and interpret information in a way that confirms their pre-existing beliefs, and anchoring bias, where decisions are influenced by initial pieces of information presented. Overcoming cognitive biases requires self-awareness, critical thinking, and the willingness to challenge one's own assumptions and beliefs.

IV. Role of Uncertainty:

Uncertainty is another factor that contributes to the

difficulty of finding solutions. Many problems are characterized by ambiguity, incomplete information, and unpredictable outcomes. Uncertainty can arise from various sources, such as technological advancements, changing socio-political contexts, or natural and environmental factors.

Uncertainty can make decision-making and problem-solving processes challenging as it introduces risks, unknowns, and potential unforeseen consequences. Decision-makers often have to grapple with trade-offs, assess probabilities, and consider long-term implications when confronted with uncertainty. Effective strategies for dealing with uncertainty include scenario planning, risk analysis, and adaptive management approaches.

V. Complexity of Global Issues:

Global issues, such as climate change, poverty, or nuclear proliferation, present a particularly complex and challenging landscape for finding solutions. These issues transcend national boundaries, involve multiple actors and stakeholders, and require international cooperation and coordination.

Global issues often require long-term planning, multilateral negotiations, and the balancing of diverse interests and priorities among nations. They also involve complex scientific, economic, and social dimensions that demand interdisciplinary approaches and collaborative efforts.

The difficulty of finding solutions stems from the complexity of problems, conflicting interests, cognitive biases, and the presence of uncertainty. Resolving complex issues requires a combination of analytical skills, effective communication, negotiation, and the ability to navigate diverse perspectives and interests. Embracing innovative approaches, fostering collaboration, and recognizing the limitations of individual perspectives are crucial steps in overcoming these difficulties in order to find effective and sustainable solutions. It is important to acknowledge that finding solutions is often an iterative process that requires continuous learning, adaptation, and the willingness to reassess and adjust strategies as new information becomes available.

Addressing the difficulty of finding solutions requires a multi-faceted approach. First and foremost, it is important to foster a culture of open dialogue, where diverse perspectives and ideas are encouraged and respected. This can help to challenge preconceived notions, break down barriers, and promote creative thinking.

Collaboration and cooperation among stakeholders are essential. Bringing together individuals, groups, organizations, and governments with different expertise and interests can lead to more comprehensive and innovative solutions. Engaging in constructive dialogue, active listening, and finding common ground can help bridge the gaps between conflicting interests and build consensus.

Furthermore, it is crucial to invest in education and capacity building. Enhancing critical thinking skills, promoting interdisciplinary learning, and cultivating a deep understanding of complex issues can empower individuals and communities to contribute to finding solutions. This includes fostering a scientific literacy that allows people to navigate and evaluate information objectively.

In addition, effective leadership plays a significant role in finding solutions. Leaders who prioritize transparency, inclusivity, and accountability can inspire and mobilize individuals and organizations towards common goals. They can also facilitate the creation of frameworks, policies, and institutions that support collaborative problem-solving and provide a platform for the exchange of ideas and expertise.

Finally, it is important to recognize that finding solutions is an ongoing process. Solutions may need to be adapted and refined over time as new challenges and opportunities arise. Monitoring and evaluation mechanisms can help assess the effectiveness of implemented solutions and identify areas for improvement.

The difficulty of finding solutions arises from the complexity of problems, conflicting interests, cognitive biases, and the presence of uncertainty. However, by embracing a holistic and collaborative approach, engaging in open dialogue, challenging cognitive biases, and investing in education and leadership, it is possible to navigate these challenges and find effective solutions. Ultimately, finding solutions requires perseverance, adaptability, and a commitment to the collective well-being of individuals, communities, and the global society.

Urgent Need for Continued Research and Dialogue

The urgent need for continued research and dialogue is a pressing issue in various domains, ranging from scientific advancements to social and political challenges. Research and dialogue serve as vital tools for expanding knowledge, fostering innovation, and addressing complex problems facing humanity. This essay will delve into the significance of continued research and dialogue, highlighting their importance in driving progress, promoting understanding, and finding sustainable solutions.

I. Advancing Knowledge and Innovation:

Continued research is crucial for advancing knowledge and pushing the boundaries of human understanding. It serves as the foundation for scientific discoveries, technological advancements, and intellectual growth. Through research, scientists and scholars explore uncharted territories, challenge existing theories, and uncover new insights that contribute to the overall progress of society.

Research plays a fundamental role in various fields, such as medicine, engineering, environmental sciences, social sciences, and humanities. It leads to the development of new treatments, technologies, policies, and strategies that address societal needs and improve the quality of life. Continued research ensures that knowledge keeps evolving, leading to innovative solutions and breakthroughs in various disciplines.

II. Tackling Complex Challenges:

The world faces numerous complex challenges, including climate change, global health crises, economic inequality, social injustice, and geopolitical conflicts. Addressing these challenges requires a deep understanding of their root causes, dynamics, and potential solutions. Research serves as a critical tool for studying and analyzing these challenges, providing insights into their multifaceted nature and guiding effective interventions.

Dialogue complements research by fostering an exchange of ideas, perspectives, and expertise among stakeholders. It brings together diverse voices, including researchers, policymakers, practitioners, and community members, to collectively understand and tackle complex challenges. Through dialogue, different perspectives can be shared, conflicting viewpoints can be addressed, and collaborative solutions can be developed.

III. Promoting Understanding and Empathy:

Research and dialogue contribute to promoting understanding and empathy among individuals and communities. Research provides a platform for exploring different cultures, histories, and experiences, fostering cross-cultural understanding and promoting diversity and inclusion. It enables researchers to investigate societal issues from multiple angles and uncover the underlying causes of social divisions and conflicts.

Dialogue, on the other hand, creates spaces for open and respectful conversations where individuals can share their experiences, perspectives, and aspirations. It helps build bridges between people of different backgrounds and ideologies, fostering empathy, tolerance, and respect for diverse opinions. Through dialogue, stereotypes can be challenged, misconceptions can be corrected, and common ground can be found, leading to greater social cohesion and harmony.

IV. Finding Sustainable Solutions:

Complex problems, such as climate change, poverty, and public health crises, require innovative and sustainable solutions. Continued research provides the necessary evidence base to identify the root causes of these issues, assess the effectiveness of existing interventions, and propose new strategies for improvement. Research helps in understanding the interconnectedness of these problems and their impacts on different sectors and communities.

Dialogue complements research by bringing together stakeholders from various sectors, including government, civil society, academia, and the private sector, to collectively address these challenges. Through dialogue, diverse perspectives can be integrated, and collaborative strategies can be developed, ensuring that solutions are comprehensive, inclusive, and sustainable. Dialogue also facilitates the identification of trade-offs, consensus building, and the mobilization of resources necessary for effective implementation.

V. Navigating Ethical Considerations:

Research and dialogue must be guided by ethical considerations to ensure the responsible and inclusive pursuit of knowledge and understanding. Ethical research practices involve respecting the rights and dignity of participants, ensuring informed consent, and safeguarding privacy and confidentiality. Dialogue should prioritize open and respectful communication, acknowledging and valuing the perspectives and experiences of all participants.

Ethical considerations also include addressing power imbalances, ensuring equitable access to research opportunities, and considering the potential impact of research and dialogue on marginalized communities. Ethical guidelines and protocols provide frameworks for researchers and participants to navigate potential ethical dilemmas and ensure that research and dialogue uphold the principles of fairness, respect, and justice.

VI. Fostering Collaboration and Partnerships:

Continued research and dialogue foster collaboration and

partnerships among different stakeholders. In an increasingly interconnected and interdependent world, no single entity can address complex challenges in isolation. Research and dialogue create opportunities for interdisciplinary collaboration, bringing together experts from diverse fields to combine their knowledge, skills, and perspectives.

Collaborative research projects leverage the expertise of multiple disciplines, leading to innovative solutions that would not be possible through isolated efforts. Dialogue platforms facilitate the exchange of ideas, the sharing of resources, and the pooling of efforts to address common goals. Collaborative approaches promote synergy, efficiency, and shared ownership of research and solutions, enhancing their effectiveness and impact.

VII. Enhancing Policy-making and Decision-making:

Research and dialogue play a crucial role in informing policy-making and decision-making processes. Rigorous and evidence-based research provides policymakers with valuable insights, data, and analysis to support informed decision-making. It helps identify effective policy interventions, assess the potential impacts of different options, and evaluate the outcomes of existing policies and programs.

Dialogue complements research by bringing together stakeholders with diverse perspectives, including policymakers, experts, affected communities, and civil society organizations. Through dialogue, policymakers can gain a deeper understanding of the concerns, needs, and aspirations of different groups, leading to more inclusive and responsive policy decisions. Dialogue also enhances transparency, accountability, and public trust in decision-making processes.

VIII. Addressing Disparities and Inequities:

Research and dialogue have the power to address disparities and inequities by highlighting social injustices and advocating for change. Research can uncover systemic biases, discrimination, and unequal access to resources, leading to a better understanding of the root causes of social inequalities. It provides evidence to support policy reforms, social programs, and interventions aimed at reducing disparities and promoting social justice.

Dialogue enables marginalized and underrepresented groups to voice their concerns, share their experiences, and participate in decision-making processes. It creates opportunities for dialogue between those who hold power and those who are affected by power imbalances. Through dialogue, solutions can be co-created, policies can be reformed, and collective action can be mobilized to address systemic inequities and promote social inclusion.

IX. Adapting to a Changing World:

The world is constantly evolving, and new challenges and opportunities arise with each passing day. Continued research and dialogue are essential to adapt to these changes and proactively address emerging issues. Research helps identify emerging trends, anticipate future challenges, and develop innovative approaches to navigate uncertainty.

Dialogue allows for the exchange of ideas and perspectives, enabling stakeholders to collectively analyze emerging issues, discuss potential implications, and explore opportunities for collaboration. Through research and dialogue, societies can stay ahead of the curve, adapt to new realities, and find sustainable solutions to emerging challenges.

Conclusion:

The urgent need for continued research and dialogue is undeniable in today's complex and interconnected world. Research drives progress, expands knowledge, and provides evidence-based solutions to address societal challenges. Dialogue fosters understanding, empathy, and collaboration, ensuring that diverse perspectives are heard and integrated into decision-making processes.

Research and dialogue are not isolated endeavors but rather interconnected and mutually reinforcing. They provide complementary approaches to tackle complex problems, promote inclusive and sustainable solutions, and address disparities and inequities. By embracing continued research and dialogue, we can foster a more informed, inclusive, and equitable world, where solutions to pressing issues are developed collaboratively, and the collective well-being of humanity is prioritized.

Summary

The complexity of nuclear politics arises from the numerous interconnected issues and challenges associated with the production, possession, and use of nuclear weapons and technology. This complexity has significant implications for global security, peace, and stability. Understanding the complexity of nuclear politics is essential to promoting effective dialogue, developing robust policies and strategies, and addressing key challenges.

Action points

1. **Promote dialogue and cooperation:** Foster open and transparent communication among nuclear-weapon states and non-nuclear-weapon states to prevent misunderstandings, misperceptions, and the escalation of tensions.

2. **Strengthen non-proliferation measures:** Develop

and enforce effective non-proliferation measures to prevent the spread of nuclear weapons and the associated risks of conflicts, terrorism, and unauthorized use.

3. **Enhance arms control agreements:** Negotiate and update arms control agreements to reflect evolving security concerns and technological advancements and address challenges and obstacles to arms control.

4. **Promote diplomacy and peaceful resolution of disputes:** Use effective diplomacy and dialogue to address disagreements, clarify positions, and seek common ground, and contribute to de-escalating tensions, defusing crises, and fostering cooperation.

5. **Foster a culture of cooperative security:** Explore alternative security paradigms and approaches that prioritize cooperative security, conflict prevention, and the addressing of underlying causes of conflicts.

Chapter 7

Summary of the Book's Content and Main Arguments

The essay *"Whispers of War: The Untold Stories Behind Nuclear Politics - The Art of War or the Art of Diplomacy"* explores the multifaceted nature of nuclear politics and examines the different dimensions, challenges, and implications it presents in the international arena.

In the historical context and evolution of nuclear politics, the essay discusses how the development of nuclear weapons during **World War II** and the subsequent *Cold War* between the *United States* and the *Soviet Union* shaped global security dynamics. It highlights the fear of *mutually assured destruction (MAD)* and the policy of deterrence as key concepts during this era.

The essay also delves into the role of nuclear weapons in ensuring national security. It explores the arguments put forth by states possessing nuclear weapons, who claim that these capabilities act as deterrents against potential adversaries and help maintain peace. However, it acknowledges the controversy surrounding nuclear weapons, with critics arguing that their possession and reliance create a precarious security environment and introduce complexities and uncertainties.

Another crucial aspect of nuclear politics covered in the essay is nuclear non-proliferation and arms control. It explains the significance of initiatives such as the Treaty on the *Non-Proliferation of Nuclear Weapons (NPT)* in preventing the spread of nuclear weapons and promoting disarmament. It also discusses arms control agreements and treaties, such as the *Strategic Arms Reduction Treaty (START)*, which limit the number of deployed strategic nuclear weapons and enhance transparency and verification measures.

The peaceful use of nuclear energy and the associated non-proliferation concerns are explored as well. The essay acknowledges the desire of many countries to harness nuclear energy for economic development but highlights the dual-use nature of nuclear technology, which raises concerns about the proliferation of nuclear weapons. It emphasizes the need for effective nonproliferation measures, including rigorous inspections, export controls, and international cooperation.

The essay also touches upon the concept of nuclear disarmament and the Global Zero movement, which advocates for the complete elimination of nuclear weapons. It highlights the steps and multilateral efforts proposed by this movement to achieve this objective.

Overall, the essay provides a comprehensive overview of nuclear politics, highlighting the complexities, challenges, and implications associated with nuclear weapons, non-proliferation efforts, arms control, peaceful use of nuclear energy, and the pursuit of nuclear disarmament. It presents different perspectives and arguments within the field and emphasizes the need for continued dialogue and research to address these critical issues.

Importance of Continued Discussion and Action on Nuclear Politics

Continued discussion and action on nuclear politics are of paramount importance due to the significant implications of nuclear weapons and technology on global security, peace, and stability. The complexities and challenges associated with nuclear politics necessitate ongoing dialogue and concerted efforts to address key issues, promote non-proliferation, strengthen arms control measures, and advance disarmament goals. This essay will delve into the importance of continued discussion and action on nuclear politics, highlighting its significance in maintaining international security, preventing nuclear proliferation, promoting diplomacy, and fostering a safer world.

I. Maintaining International Security:

One of the primary reasons for continued discussion and action on nuclear politics is to maintain international security. The possession and potential use of nuclear weapons by states pose significant risks and threats to global peace and stability. Engaging in dialogue and collaborative efforts allows countries to address security concerns, build trust, and establish mechanisms for crisis management and conflict resolution.

Open and transparent communication among nuclear-weapon states and non-nuclear-weapon states is essential to prevent misunderstandings, misperceptions, and the escalation of tensions. Through ongoing discussions, countries can express their security concerns, clarify intentions, and work towards building a more stable and secure international environment.

II. Preventing Nuclear Proliferation:

Continued discussion and action on nuclear politics are critical in preventing the proliferation of nuclear weapons. The proliferation of these weapons to additional states or non-state actors significantly increases the risks of nuclear conflicts, terrorism, and unauthorized use. By engaging in dialogue and international cooperation, countries can develop and enforce effective non-proliferation measures.

The *Treaty on the Non-Proliferation of Nuclear Weapons (NPT)* serves as a key international framework to prevent the spread of nuclear weapons. Ongoing discussions and actions are necessary to strengthen the implementation of the treaty, encourage universal adherence, and address emerging challenges. Additionally, continued dialogue allows for the sharing of best practices, expertise, and information on non-proliferation efforts, ensuring that states are equipped to detect and counter illicit nuclear activities.

III. Strengthening Arms Control Measures:

Dialogue and action on nuclear politics are vital for strengthening arms control measures and promoting disarmament. Arms control agreements and treaties, such as *START*, provide mechanisms for reducing nuclear arsenals, enhancing transparency, and promoting confidence-building measures between nuclear-weapon states.

Continued discussions enable states to negotiate and update these agreements to reflect evolving security concerns and technological advancements. Moreover, sustained dialogue can address challenges and obstacles to arms control, such as the development of new delivery systems, emerging technologies, and the modernization of existing nuclear arsenals.

IV. Promoting Diplomacy and Conflict Resolution:

Nuclear politics often involve complex diplomatic negotiations and require effective conflict resolution mechanisms. Dialogue plays a central role in promoting diplomacy and peaceful resolution of disputes related to nuclear issues. By engaging in ongoing discussions, countries can address disagreements, clarify positions, and seek common ground.

Effective diplomacy and dialogue can contribute to

de-escalating tensions, defusing crises, and fostering cooperation among nuclear-armed states. It provides a platform for exploring diplomatic solutions, including confidence-building measures, arms control agreements, and regional security arrangements.

V. Fostering a Safer World:

Ultimately, continued discussion and action on nuclear politics aim to foster a safer world. Nuclear weapons present existential threats, and the consequences of their use would be catastrophic. By engaging in ongoing dialogue and collective action, the international community can work towards reducing the risks associated with nuclear weapons, mitigating the dangers of accidental or unauthorized use, and creating conditions conducive to disarmament.

Dialogue also allows for the exploration of alternative security paradigms and approaches that prioritize cooperative security, conflict prevention, and the addressing of underlying causes of conflicts.

By fostering a culture of dialogue and cooperation, countries can build trust, enhance mutual understanding, and promote shared security

VI. Addressing Emerging Challenges:

Continued discussion and action on nuclear politics are essential for addressing emerging challenges and developments in the field. The rapid advancement of technology and the evolving geopolitical landscape pose new risks and complexities to nuclear security. Ongoing dialogue allows for the identification and assessment of these challenges, enabling timely and effective responses.

Issues such as cyber threats, the potential militarization of outer space, and the development of hypersonic weapons require sustained dialogue and cooperation among nations. By engaging in discussions, countries can exchange information, share expertise, and develop strategies to mitigate these emerging risks and ensure the resilience of nuclear systems.

VII. Engaging Civil Society and Public Awareness:

Continued discussion on nuclear politics also involves engaging civil society and raising public awareness about the implications of nuclear weapons and the importance of disarmament. Nuclear issues are not limited to policymakers and experts alone; they have far-reaching consequences for global citizens.

Through dialogue and action, governments, non-governmental organizations, and academic institutions can facilitate public engagement, promote education on nuclear issues, and encourage informed discussions. Public participation in nuclear politics fosters accountability, strengthens democratic processes, and empowers individuals to advocate for peaceful solutions and disarmament.

VIII. Multilateral Cooperation and Trust-Building:

Multilateral cooperation and trust-building are vital components of continued discussion and action on nuclear politics. Nuclear issues affect all nations, and no single country can effectively address these challenges alone. By engaging in ongoing dialogue and cooperative efforts, countries can build trust, strengthen relationships, and foster a sense of collective responsibility.

International forums and organizations such as the United Nations, the *International Atomic Energy Agency (IAEA)*, and the *Comprehensive Nuclear-Test-Ban Treaty Organization (CTBTO)* provide platforms for multilateral cooperation on nuclear issues. Continued discussion within these frameworks facilitates the exchange of information, coordination of efforts, and the establishment of norms and standards.

IX. Safeguarding the Future Generations:

The importance of continued discussion and action on nuclear politics lies in safeguarding the future generations. The consequences of nuclear conflicts or accidents can have long-lasting effects on human lives, the environment, and the well-being of future generations. By actively engaging in dialogue and taking concrete actions, nations can work towards reducing nuclear risks and creating a safer world for generations to come.

Dialogue and action on nuclear politics demonstrate a commitment to the principles of disarmament, non-proliferation, and peaceful resolution of conflicts. It sets a precedent for future generations, emphasizing the responsibility of current leaders to ensure the security and well-being of future societies.

The importance of continued discussion and action on nuclear politics cannot be overstated. Engaging in ongoing dialogue and concerted efforts is essential for maintaining international security, preventing nuclear proliferation, promoting diplomacy, and fostering a safer world. By addressing emerging challenges, engaging civil society, and promoting multilateral cooperation, nations can work interests. This, in turn, can help to reduce tensions, prevent conflicts, and promote regional stability.

Summary

The last two topics addressed in the essay are *"Importance of continued discussion and action on nuclear politics"* and *"Fostering a safer world."* The summary encompasses the key points discussed in both sections. In the first topic, the importance of continued discussion and action on nuclear politics was highlighted, emphasizing the significance of ongoing dialogue and concerted efforts in addressing key issues, promoting non-proliferation, strengthening arms control measures, and advancing disarmament goals. The complexities and challenges associated with nuclear politics require sustained engagement and collaboration to ensure international security, prevent nuclear proliferation, and promote diplomacy.

The second topic focused on fostering a safer world through continued discussion and action on nuclear politics. It emphasized the need to mitigate the risks associated with nuclear weapons, prevent conflicts, and create conditions conducive to disarmament. Diplomacy and conflict resolution were highlighted as critical tools in de-escalating tensions, promoting cooperation, and exploring alternative security paradigms that prioritize shared security interests.

Action words

1. **Engage:** It signifies the importance of actively participating in dialogue and collaborative efforts on nuclear politics to address key challenges and promote peace and security.

2. **Strengthen:** It emphasizes the need to reinforce arms control measures, non-proliferation efforts, and diplomatic mechanisms to enhance global security and stability.

3. **Prevent:** It highlights the necessity of taking proactive steps to prevent nuclear proliferation, conflicts, and the unauthorized

use of nuclear weapons.

4. **Promote:** It signifies the active promotion of diplomacy, cooperation, and conflict resolution to foster peaceful resolutions and reduce tensions in nuclear politics.

5. **Mitigate:** It underscores the importance of taking measures to reduce the risks associated with nuclear weapons, including accidental or unauthorized use, through collective action and international cooperation.

Special Bonus

SPECIAL BONUS!

Want These 2 Bonus EBooks For Free?

Get FREE, Unlimited Access To These and All of Our New Books By Joining Our Community

CLICK HERE TO JOIN

Thank You!

Thank you for taking the time to check out my work - I hope you enjoy reading it as much as I enjoyed writing it! Authors wouldn't be anywhere without readers like you, so your support **REALLY** means a lot. I'm a firm believer that books don't need to be expensive or difficult to get hold of - so I want to encourage **EVERYONE** to enjoy the pleasure of books - and not just mine.

<u>I would be grateful if you could **WRITE ME A REVIEW** on the product detail page about how this book has helped you. Your review means a lot to me, as I would love to hear about your successes.</u>
Nothing makes me happier than knowing that my work has aided someone in achieving their goals and progressing in life; which would likewise motivate me to improve and serve you better, and also encourage other readers to get influenced positively by my work.
<u>Your feedback means so much to me, and I will never take it for granted.</u>

I'd love to hear from you if you have any recommendations

of your own, so please do get in touch if you've read anything awesome lately.

If you ever have any questions, you can get in touch at sam@samamoo.com.

I want you to enjoy your reading experience; your satisfaction is my number one priority. You are well appreciated for reading this book.

Thank you, have a wonderful day!

About The Author

I am a dynamic entrepreneur, visionary founder, and accomplished author with a passion for empowering individuals and businesses to achieve unparalleled success. With a proven track record of leadership and innovation, I have established myself as a prominent figure in the realms of entrepreneurship, publishing, and business coaching.

My professional journey has been defined by a relentless pursuit of excellence and a steadfast commitment to delivering tangible results. I take great pride in my ability to seamlessly blend strategic planning, meticulous coordination, and adept implementation of best practices to orchestrate transformative protocols and methodologies. This proficiency has consistently led to noteworthy advancements in both quality and operational processes, catalyzing organizations toward the realization of their overarching objectives.

One of my distinguishing strengths lies in my strategic acumen, which has enabled me to navigate through market shifts and anticipate emerging trends and technologies. I have a knack for identifying opportunities and harnessing innovation to enrich enterprises with substantial value. Furthermore, my reputation as a prolific content creator and publisher is underscored by my authorship of impactful books and articles spanning business, personal development, and technology. My writing prowess shines through in my ability to concisely convey intricate concepts, making them accessible to diverse audiences.

Connect with me here:

Instagram: https://instagram.com/_amoosam

Facebook: https://fb.me/samamoo.official

Twitter: https://twitter.com/samamooofficial

LinkedIn: https://www.linkedin.com/company/samamoo

Email: sam@samamoo.com

Website: https://samamoo.com

Other Books

- How to be More in Tune with The Feelings of Your Customers
- Time Management For Busy People
- Sell Like titans

www.ingramcontent.com/pod-product-compliance
Lightning Source LLC
Chambersburg PA
CBHW072152070526
44585CB00015B/1105